Ukulele
for Beginners

Ukulele
for Beginners

TOM FLEMING

amber
BOOKS

Published by
Amber Books Ltd
74–77 White Lion Street
London
N1 9PF
United Kingdom
www.amberbooks.co.uk
Appstore: itunes.com/apps/amberbooksltd
Facebook: www.facebook.com/amberbooks
Twitter: @amberbooks

ISBN: 978-1-78274-518-1

Project Editor: Sarah Uttridge
Consultant: Mark Batley
Designer: Brian Rust
Picture Research: Terry Forshaw

Printed in China

CONTENTS

Introduction

INTRODUCTION

The ukulele (or 'uke') has experienced a surge in popularity in recent years across a range of styles. It is a great instrument in many situations, from schools to pub sing-alongs, and is often used in pop record production to replace or augment guitar-based textures, giving an instantly sparkly, 'happy' sound. This book is intended to help you with your first steps as a budding ukulele player.

Taylor Swift
Taylor Swift is as proficient on the ukulele as she is on the guitar – as a result the uke's image has received a significant boost.

Cavaquinho
This small stringed instrument is very similar to the modern ukulele, though the tuning is different

This book is divided into chapters covering various skills and areas of knowledge that any uke player needs in order to get started on the instrument. Beyond this, there is a whole world of uke players and music to explore. Current ukulele players tend to be young and heavily focused on social media, making it very easy to make new discoveries and stay abreast of developments.

HISTORY

Though it may look like a small guitar, the ukulele is in fact more like a cousin than a direct descendant. The ukulele is directly related to various small, guitar-like instruments introduced to Hawaii by Portuguese immigrants in the nineteenth century, including the machete and the cavaquinho. The latter is very similar to the ukulele, and features prominently in both Portuguese and Brazilian music. The main difference between the ukulele and the cavaquinho is that the cavaquinho has metal strings and is tuned differently, so the available range of chords and sounds is different too.

Some of the ideas discussed in this book will be familiar if you are coming to the ukulele from the guitar, but some aspects (such as tuning) are unique to the uke. Whereas most guitar players use a pick (plectrum), on the uke the situation is reversed: most players use their fingers, though we will discuss pick technique briefly too.

POSTURE AND TECHNIQUE

The uke's shape and small size make it perfect for any number of playing situations and equally easy to play whether sitting or standing. We will cover the basics of both left- and right-hand technique; the most important aspect of this is all parts of the body should remain relaxed. If any part feels tense, you are probably trying too hard!

PRACTICE AND USING THIS BOOK

This book contains a variety of exercises to help you along the way as you learn new chords and techniques, as well as popular songs to put them fully into practice. Beyond this, a large number of resources can be used. By the end of this book you will have learned enough to be able to find any common chord, in any key, so any sheet music or internet resource that uses chord symbols (whether intended for uke, guitar or other instruments) can be used.

We've also added some information on important and inspirational ukulele players, from the early twentieth century to the present day. Listening to

Technique

Most serious uke players use the fingers rather than a pick. This right-hand position is perfect for relaxed strumming and most fingerpicking styles.

their music and investigating online resources related to their playing styles will help you progress in any direction that appeals to you.

Finally, the Chords Reference section provides a handy reference point that should help you get through most songs that you might want to play on the ukulele.

Customize your uke

Ukes are available in many different designs. Some companies even offer custom graphics – you can even upload your own image when ordering.

CHAPTER 1:

UKULELE BASICS

This chapter guides you through the basics of choosing a uke and other accessories, tuning, posture, the left-hand and right-hand technique and playing your very first chord.

LEFT: Taimane Gardner has the ability to play all musical genres, from classical to rock to flamenco.

WHAT YOU NEED

You can get started with just a ukulele and a tuner. However, a few other items will make life easier and help you get the most from your instrument.

UKULELE
(PP. 12–13)

PICKS/ PLECTRA
(PP. 14–15)

TUNER
(PP. 20–21)

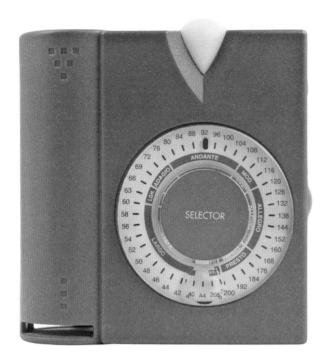

METRONOME
(P. 25)

STRING WINDER/ TRIMMER
(P. 42)

SPARE STRINGS
(PP. 42–43)

D'ADDARIO™

Ukulele

MADE IN USA

✧ STRINGS ✧

J65 • Clear Nylon
1st-.024, 2nd-.032, 3rd-.034, 4th-.028

STRAP*
(P. 15)

* NOT COMPATIBLE WITH ALL UKULELES

11

CHOOSING A UKULELE

There is a whole family of ukuleles available in various sizes, from the smallest (sopranino) to the largest (bass). By far the most common is the soprano or standard ukulele, which is the second smallest instrument in the family.

Sizes
Ukuleles from left to right: Baritone, tenor, concert and soprano.

PRICE VARIATIONS

Ukuleles vary in price and quality, from extremely cheap instruments to much more serious and expensive ones. You can get started with any of them, but it is worth spending a little more than the bare minimum, as the very cheapest ukes can be difficult to keep in tune.

Soprano
The soprano ukulele is the most popular. The very cheapest ukes are sopranos, but higher-quality instruments are also available.

The cheapest instruments tend to have simple wooden or plastic tuning pegs that can easily slip, causing tuning errors. If possible, try to find an instrument with guitar-style tuning pegs, also known as machine heads.

The most basic ukes are made of plywood or even plastic. More expensive instruments are usually made of genuine wood, giving them a fuller tone and greater volume.

Tenor
The tenor uke is normally tuned re-entrant (see re-entrant Tuning, p. 21), but it can be retuned with a low G string for an alternative chord shape.

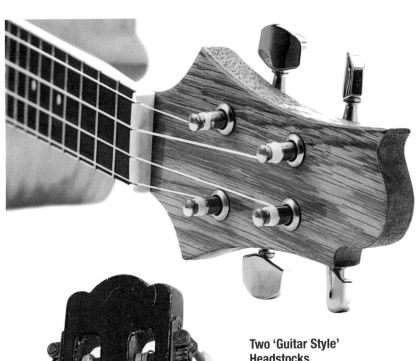

Concert
The concert ukulele is usually tuned the same way as the soprano, but offers a bigger, fuller tone. A concert uke may be easier to play if you have large hands.

Two 'Guitar Style' Headstocks
Above: Acoustic guitar style. This offers stable tuning and ease of use.

Left: Classical guitar style. This type also offers stable tuning. Some players prefer the look, but re-stringing may take a little longer.

CONCERT UKULELE

If you have a little more money to spend, you may want to consider a concert ukulele. This is slightly larger than the soprano, and usually of a higher build quality than the cheapest sopranos. As well as being easier to play if you have large hands, a concert uke will generally give a fuller sound and more reliable tuning.

UKE VARIETIES

Almost everything in this book can be applied to any model of ukulele, although some ideas will sound slightly different on a tenor or baritone without re-entrant tuning (see p. 21).

ACCESSORIES

You won't need much in the way of accessories when you're just getting started on the ukulele: a handful of inexpensive items will help you get the most from your new instrument.

Tuner
Clip tuners like this one are inexpensive and convenient. Many players leave one in place permanently.

Headstock

TUNER

There are many ways to tune a ukulele or other fretted instrument; modern digital tuners are usually the best option as they are highly accurate yet inexpensive. Tuners are available in many shapes and sizes, including pocket ones the size of a credit card and even smaller versions. Clip-on tuners are increasingly popular; these attach to the instrument's headstock and pick up vibrations directly from the instrument rather than from the air.

Almost all modern tuners are suitable for tuning a ukulele. Just check that it is a chromatic tuner, or at least has a chromatic mode, as some dedicated guitar tuners will only tune to the standard pitches of guitar strings. A chromatic tuner covers all other notes too, making it suitable for all ukulele tunings.

PICKS

Uke strings are made of soft nylon, so many players use their fingers alone to strum or pick. However, you may also wish to use a pick (plectrum), particularly if you are coming to the ukulele from the guitar and you are accustomed to this technique.

Picks come in various shapes, sizes and thicknesses. Generally, medium or light picks work best for the ukulele, but by all means try a few different gauges as you progress on the instrument.

While standard guitar picks are perfectly usable, many uke players prefer picks made of felt, as they give a warmer and less 'clicky' sound.

Picks
A selection of picks. Try a few different types to see what works for you, but don't forget to try using your fingers without the pick too.

TUNER APPS

You may not need a dedicated tuner: if you have a smartphone, you can choose from a range of free or inexpensive tuner apps.

www.stones-music.co.uk

Strap

Various kinds of strap are available. Most of them look something like this as many ukes, unlike guitars, don't have strap fixings.

STRAP

The ukulele is a small and light instrument, so many players find that there is no need for a strap, even when standing – and many ukes have no strap fixings. However, some more expensive instruments do have dedicated strap fixings; some straps attach to the headstock and soundhole, as shown above.

CASE

If you are going to travel anywhere with your uke, you will need a case of some sort. For inexpensive instruments a soft case will usually suffice. If you have made a bigger investment, or you are planning to travel a lot, a hard case may be worth considering.

Soft and Hard Cases

If you are planning to travel with your uke, even just to local gigs, a case is essential. Because of their size, even hard cases are generally not expensive.

ANATOMY OF THE UKE

The ukulele is a lot like an acoustic guitar in terms of general construction. If you are not familiar with the parts of a guitar, it may be useful to study the diagram shown here for future reference.

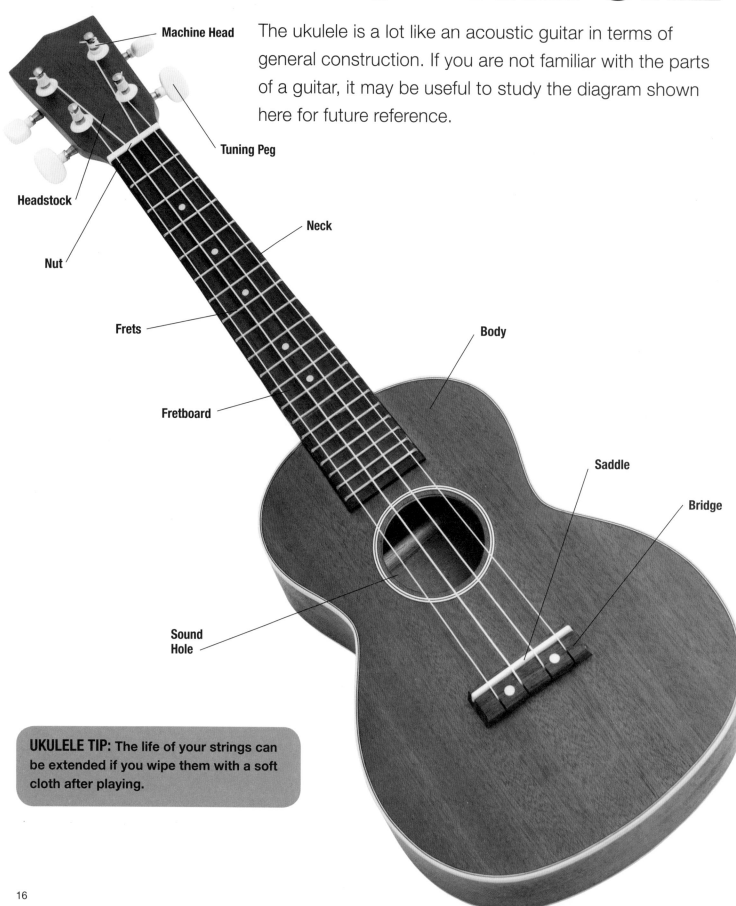

Machine Head

Tuning Peg

Headstock

Nut

Neck

Frets

Body

Fretboard

Saddle

Bridge

Sound Hole

UKULELE TIP: The life of your strings can be extended if you wipe them with a soft cloth after playing.

UKULELE VARIANTS

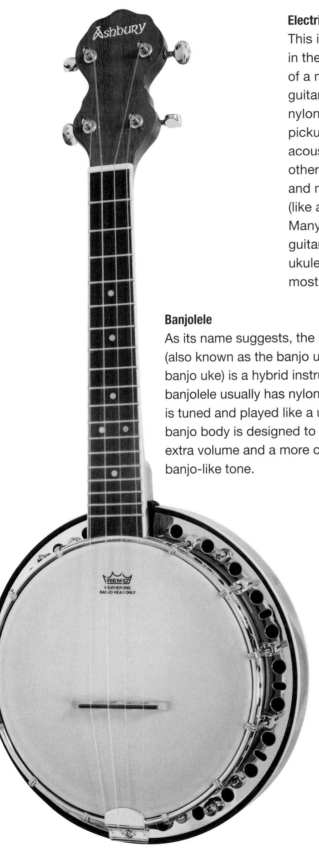

Electric Ukulele
This is essentially a ukulele in the physical format of a miniature electric guitar. Some models have nylon strings with a piezo pickup (like an electro-acoustic guitar), while others have steel strings and magnetic pickups (like an electric guitar). Many of the major electric guitar manufacturers make ukulele versions of their most iconic guitars.

Banjolele
As its name suggests, the banjolele (also known as the banjo ukulele or banjo uke) is a hybrid instrument. The banjolele usually has nylon strings and is tuned and played like a uke, but the banjo body is designed to produce extra volume and a more cutting, banjo-like tone.

Electric Uke
This electric ukulele is styled to resemble a Gibson Les Paul guitar.

POSTURE AND TECHNIQUE

The ukulele is easy to play, whether sitting or standing. If you are using a strap, this should be adjusted so that the instrument is placed somewhere around the middle of your upper body, whether sitting or standing. If you are not using a strap, aim for approximately the same height anyway.

UKULELE TIP: Throughout this book, we will use the terms 'left' and 'right' as they apply to a right-handed player. If you are left-handed, you will need a left-handed ukulele or a right-handed model strung for left-handed playing. In that case, simply reverse all occurrences of 'left' and 'right'.

THE RIGHT HAND

The right hand (assuming you are right-handed) strums or picks the strings. Strumming means playing several strings at once; picking means playing one string at a time. The pick can be used for both strumming and picking, with essentially the same technique. Many players strum using their fingernails in a relaxed motion, and pick using the nails – a bit like classical guitar.

HOLDING THE PICK

The pick is held between the thumb and index finger of the right hand. The thumb should be at approximately a right angle to the first joint of the index finger, with the pick in between. Generally only a few millimetres of the pick should protrude. Hold the pick just tightly enough to keep it in place when playing.

THE LEFT HAND

The fingers of the left hand press the strings down on to the fretboard, usually using the tip of the finger. When one string is pressed in a given place while the right hand picks the same string, a single note is produced. When the right hand strums across several strings, more than one note is produced. This is called a chord. Chords are made up of several fretted notes and/or several open strings.

The left-hand thumb should always make contact with the back of the neck. As the ukulele is a very small instrument for adult hands, the thumb may wrap around the neck to some extent; this is not a problem as long as it does not get in the way of the other fingers or stop open strings from sounding. The thumb should remain roughly behind the fingers and perpendicular to the neck, however, and should not be allowed to stray too far sideways.

The fingers of the left hand should be allowed to hover in readiness above the fretboard when not actually playing notes or chords – avoid letting them stray to the side or underneath the instrument.

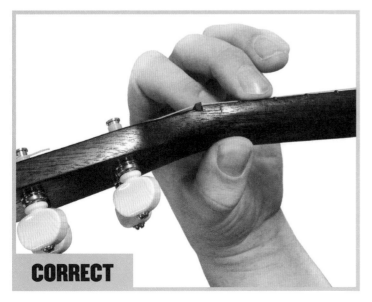

CORRECT

INCORRECT

TUNING

Always check that your uke is in tune before playing. The four strings of the soprano or standard ukulele are usually tuned to the notes G, C, E and A.

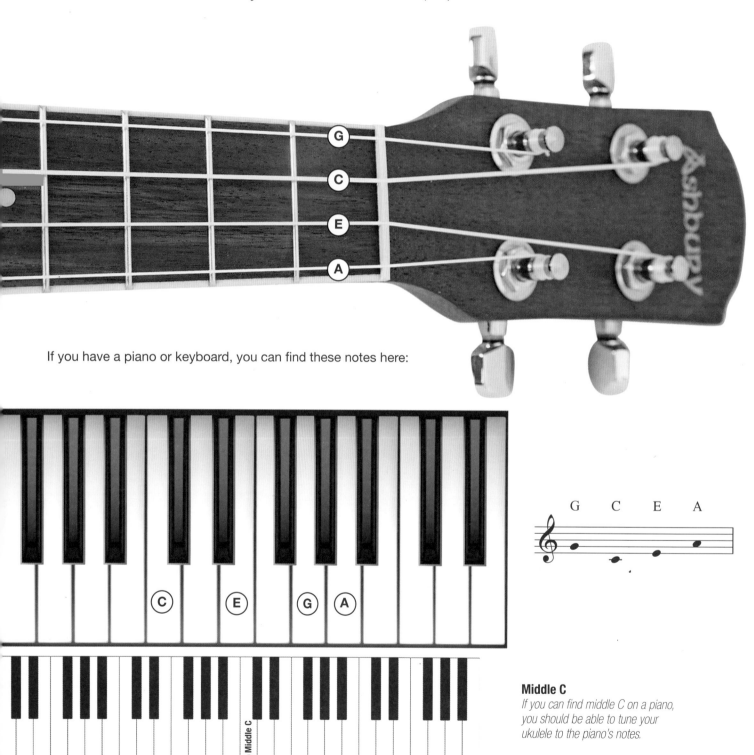

If you have a piano or keyboard, you can find these notes here:

Middle C

If you can find middle C on a piano, you should be able to tune your ukulele to the piano's notes.

RE-ENTRANT TUNING

Most stringed instruments have strings that are arranged from low to high. On fretted instruments this means that the first string you strum will be the lowest. The ukulele is different: the first string is actually higher than the next two. This contributes to the uke's unique sound. In spite of this, guitar chords still work. To be specific: the ukulele is like a four-string guitar with a capo at the fifth fret, but with the bottom string raised by an octave. If you know the chords to a song on the guitar, they can easily be used on the uke, though the key will be different — for example, the D chord on the guitar becomes a G chord on the uke.

Tuning
Here, the display shows a G, so we know we are at least close to the correct pitch. Next, check whether the display is showing that the pitch is flat (in which case we raise the pitch by tightening the string), sharp (lower the pitch by loosening the string) or perfectly in tune.

In Tune
All tuners have some way of indicating that the string is perfectly in tune. An old-fashioned needle display should be dead centre when the string is in tune. The more modern digital display, shown here, turns green when the string is in tune.

USING A TUNER

The easiest way to tune a ukulele is to use a digital tuner or clip tuner. Simply play each string in turn and adjust the pitch by turning the tuning peg until the needle or digital display shows that the string is in tune (usually dead centre in the display).

A chromatic tuner will tell you the name of the note that you are tuning. Always check that you are tuning to the correct note! At home, each string probably won't stray very far from its tuned pitch, but if you have travelled you may find that things have moved considerably; if you just look at the tuner's needle you could end up tuning to the wrong notes.

YOUR FIRST CHORD

A chord is a group of notes that sound good together. On the ukulele, a chord can contain up to four notes – one on each string – that may be either fretted notes or open strings.

CHORD BOXES

Chord boxes provide the simplest way to show how to play a chord. The box is really a grid, with four vertical lines representing the strings, and a number of horizontal lines representing frets. A thick horizontal line at the top represents the nut.

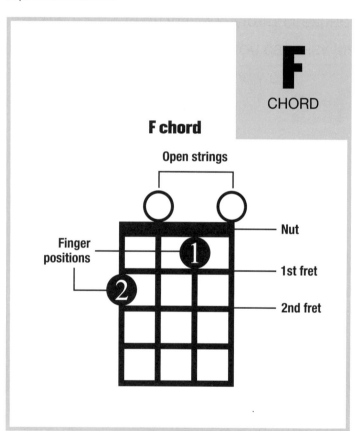

F chord

Open strings

Finger positions

Nut

1st fret

2nd fret

F CHORD

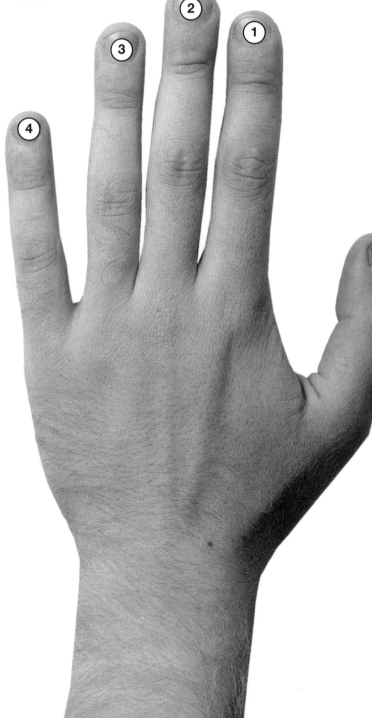

Finger Numbers
Pay attention to the finger numbers shown for all of the chords in this book.

A number of dots are used to show where to place the fingers. For beginners, these are usually numbered, so you know exactly which fingers to use.

All we need to show how to play a basic chord is a box with these finger dots, and often just a few other symbols.

If there is no fingering dot on a string, it is either because the open string is part of the chord (shown with an 'O') or because the string should not be played in this chord (shown with an 'X').

The name of the chord is shown above the box.

THE C CHORD

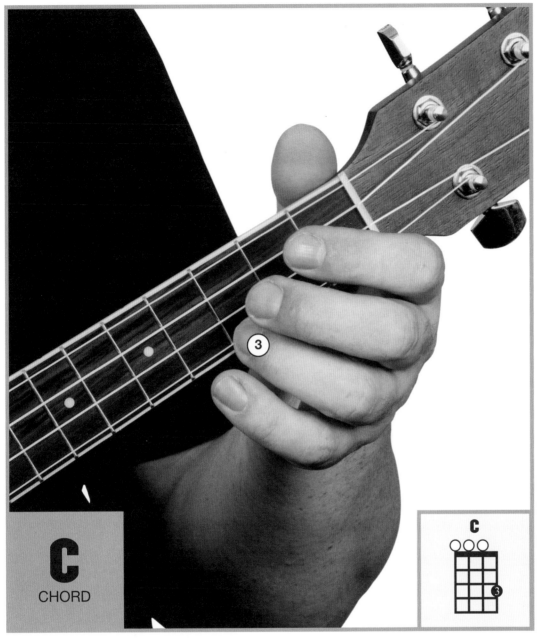

C
CHORD

C
○○○

3

STRUMMING

Almost all music has a time signature: this is the number of beats that you would have to keep counting if you were counting along to the music. In most pop and rock music, this number is four, so we keep counting '1 2 3 4, 1 2 3 4, 1 2 3 4…'. Each group of four beats is known as a bar. In written music, bars are separated using vertical lines called barlines. The symbol **4/4** at the beginning shows that there are four beats per bar.

EXERCISE 1

1. **C**

$\frac{4}{4}$ ↓ ↓ ↓ ↓ | ↓ ↓ ↓ ↓ | ↓ ↓ ↓ ↓ | ↓ ↓ ↓ ↓ :|
    1   2   3   4   1   2   3   4   1   2   3   4   1   2   3   4

STRUMMING EXERCISES

Strummed ukulele parts involve a degree of coordination: the left hand must change chord shape every so often, while the right hand provides the rhythmic interest. To start with, we'll keep the left hand holding just one chord shape while the right hand plays some simple rhythms.

The exercises on these two pages all use just the C chord.

While the time signature does not generally change within a song, this does not mean that you have to strum on every beat. In this book, we will progress gradually from very simple strumming ideas to more complex ones.

The time signatures here are either **4/4** (four beats per bar) or **3/4** (three beats per bar). Keep counting to either 4 or 3 as applicable, but strum only where shown. Where there is no strum on a beat, the chord should be allowed to sound: chords may sound for one, two, three or four beats. This creates some simple rhythms.

REPEATS

Special barlines are used to show that a section of music should be repeated. These look like double barlines with two dots on one side or other, meaning 'start of repeated section' and 'end of repeated section'.

‖:   start repeat

:‖   end repeat

‖:   (repeat this material)   :‖

EXERCISES

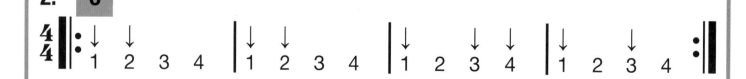

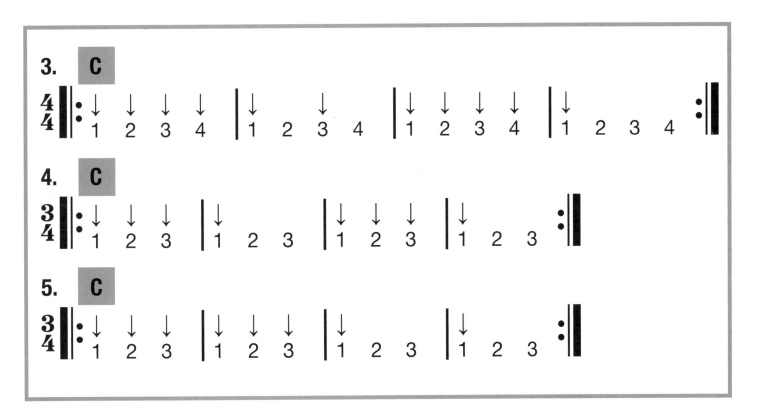

USING A METRONOME

The metronome is a convenient practice tool that makes a regular 'click' sound. Several different kinds are available, including old-fashioned mechanical types, modern digital models and smartphone apps. It is important that the pulse timing is precise and is adjustable. Usually, this speed (known in music as 'tempo') is set in beats per minute (bpm). If you have a metronome or app, try playing these exercises at a tempo setting of around 80 bpm. Try to make each strum happen at exactly the same time as each click.

Pendulum

Mechanical Metronome
These tend to be more expensive than digital ones, but some people find them more satisfying to use. In addition to the regular 'click' sound, a bell can be set to chime on the desired beat.

Digital Metronome
These tend to be cheaper and more flexible than mechanical ones; some even have a tuner built in.

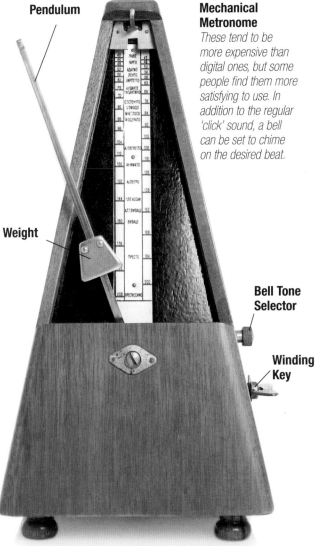

Weight

Bell Tone Selector

Winding Key

UKULELE HEROES

JAKE SHIMABUKURO

1976–

RECOMMENDED LISTENING:
Sunday Morning
Grand Ukulele

Jake Shimabukuro is a Hawaiian virtuoso ukulele player and composer. His ukulele playing spans a broad range of styles including bluegrass, folk, jazz and classical music.

Shimabukuro came to fame within Hawaii in the late 1990s with the group Pure Heart before embarking on a solo career in 2002. Having secured a contract with Sony Music in Japan, he toured extensively and built a significant following there. This was cemented by a number of Japanese-only CD releases.

In 2006, Shimabukuro became an early viral YouTube sensation with his virtuoso arrangement of The Beatles' song "While My Guitar Gently Weeps", which rapidly received several million views. Cover arrangements of this kind have since become a staple of his live act (including other Beatles songs and, famously, Queen's "Bohemian Rhapsody").

Jake Shimabukuro employs many right-hand techniques reminiscent of classical guitar and flamenco, though his music fuses these styles with jazz harmony and a rhythmic drive clearly influenced by rock music. His 2012 album *Grand Ukulele* was recorded live with a 29-piece orchestra.

Shimabukuro has composed soundtracks for two major Japanese films: *Hula Girls* and *Sideways*. He has won numerous Hawaiian Music Awards, and two of his collaborations (with Ziggy Marley and Yo-Yo Ma) have won Grammy Awards.

Tenor Ukulele
Jake Shimabukuro playing a tenor ukulele, with large right hand movement and powerful strumming technique in evidence.

FAVOURED INSTRUMENT:

**KAMAKA CUSTOM
TENOR UKULELE**

CHAPTER 2:
CHANGING CHORDS

Many songs use just a handful of chords. As well as learning the chords themselves, it is important to practise changing quickly and smoothly between them.

LEFT: Israel Kamakawiwoʻole was the most popular entertainer in Hawaii until his tragic death in 1997.

THE G CHORD

Our next chord is called G, or G major. This shape uses fingers 1, 2 and 3. The G chord is a very useful chord that can be used in several important keys on the ukulele. The G chord uses all four strings, so you don't have to worry about which strings to strum.

G
CHORD

UKULELE TIP: Most songs use three or more chords. One of these, known as the tonic chord, defines the key of the song, so we say that the song is 'in the key of G' (for example). Usually, the tonic chord will appear more often than any other chord, and generally sounds like 'home' – as though the music comes to rest when this chord is reached.

CHANGING CHORDS

The greatest challenge for the beginner is to learn to change chords without holding up the flow of the music. To begin with, practise changing from C to G in no particular rhythm. Strum the C chord, allow it to ring and then change as quickly as possible to the G chord. Pay attention to exactly what each finger needs to do to make the change, and try to make the movement as economical as possible.

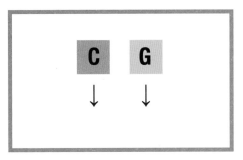

CHANGING IN TIME

Next, try to time the change so you will be ready to play the new chord at a precise point. Don't worry about strumming on every beat of the bar at this stage – one strum per bar (four beats) is enough. If you have a metronome, set it to around 80 bpm and count '1 2 3 4' for each chord. As the chord sounds, try to prepare yourself for the chord change.

    If you find this too challenging at first, try a slower tempo such as 60 bpm, or allow each chord to sound for two whole bars (8 beats) at first. (If you don't have a metronome, you can use the second hand of a watch or clock as a metronome fixed to 60 bpm.)

Once you have mastered this, move on to playing two strums per bar (beats 1 and 3).

Next, move on to playing on every beat in the bar. Don't worry at this stage if the fourth beat gets cut off as you start to change. This will get smoother as you progress, but it will never disappear entirely; there will always be small squeaks and scuffs – that's the sound of a real human being playing an instrument.

TWO NEW CHORDS: F AND Am

Thousands of songs can be played using just three chords, and even more with four. If we add two new chords to the C and G chords we have learned so far, we can play most three- and four-chord songs in the key of C.

THE F CHORD

This chord shape uses just two fingers: the first and second. Fretted strings alternate with open strings in this shape and it is important to make sure that these sound too. In particular, the open string between the two fretted strings could easily be muted accidentally. Try playing the strings one at a time while fretting this shape to make sure that all notes are sounding.

THE Am CHORD

The other three chords we have learned (C, F and G) are all major chords. If a chord name is made up of just a note name, it is a major chord even though this is not spelled out. The 'm' suffix stands for 'minor', so this new chord is actually 'A minor'. Major and minor chords sound different: in simple terms, major chords sound happy and minor chords sound sad.

CHANGING CHORDS

All of the chords we have learned so far belong together in the key of C, and might occur in any order. Practise changing between all possible combinations of these chords:

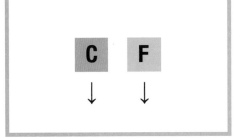

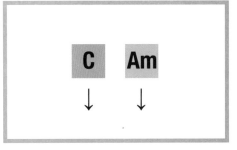

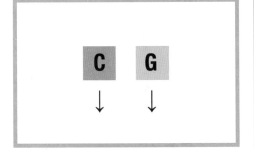

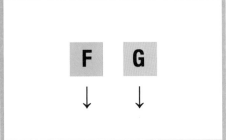

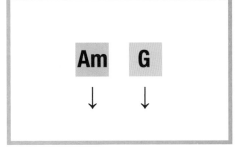

EXERCISES

These exercises are written with four strums per bar, but you may want to start by strumming once per bar, and then twice (see p. 31).

1.
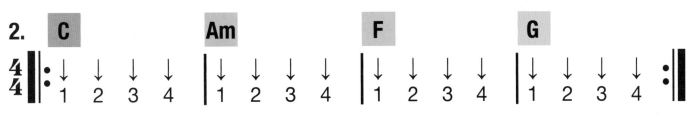

2.
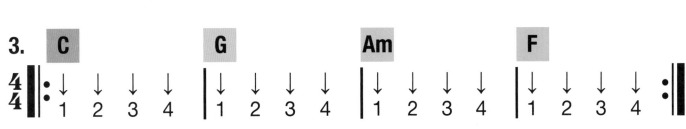

3.

PLAY A SONG

Swing Low, Sweet Chariot

This traditional spiritual song has been covered by numerous artists including Elvis Presley, Johnny Cash and Eric Clapton. It's easy to play using just three chords, and is arranged here in the key of C (chords C, F and G).

CHORDS

CHORD SEQUENCE

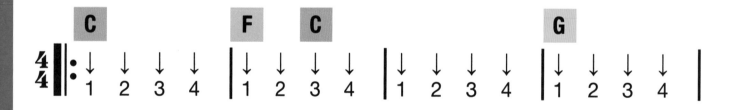

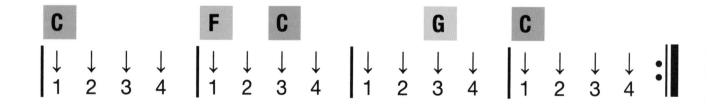

CHORUS

C   **F**   **C**
Swing low, sweet chariot

         G
Coming for to carry me home,

C   **F**   **C**
Swing low, sweet chariot,

    G   **C**
Coming for to carry me home.

VERSE 1

C   **F**   **C**
I looked over Jordan, and what did I see

       G
Coming for to carry me home?

 C   **F**   **C**
A band of angels coming after me,

     G   **C**
Coming for to carry me home.

Repeat Chorus

VERSE 2

C   **F**   **C**
Sometimes I'm up, and sometimes I'm down,

       G
(Coming for to carry me home)

   C   **F**   **C**
But still my soul feels heavenly bound.

     G   **C**
(Coming for to carry me home)

Repeat Chorus

VERSE 3

  C   **F**   **C**
The brightest day that I can say,

       G
(Coming for to carry me home)

   C   **F** **C**
When Jesus washed my sins away.

     G   **C**
(Coming for to carry me home)

Repeat Chorus

VERSE 4

C   **F**   **C**
If I get there before you do,

       G
(Coming for to carry me home)

 C   **F**   **C**
I'll cut a hole and pull you through.

    G   **C**
(Coming for to carry me home)

Repeat Chorus

VERSE 5

  C   **F** **C**
If you get there before I do,

       G
(Coming for to carry me home)

C   **F**   **C**
Tell all my friends I'm coming too.

    G   **C**
(Coming for to carry me home)

Repeat Chorus

MORE CHORDS

A few more chords are needed to help us play in most 'friendly' uke keys. Later, we will look at a way of moving these further up the neck, making all keys available (see barre chords, pp. 72–73).

THE A CHORD

This is a really easy chord using just two fingers. The A chord is important for playing in the key of D (and later you will need it for the less friendly keys of A and E). It also sounds great in D minor – try it once you have learned the D minor chord (p. 40).

E MINOR CHORD

This is an important chord in the key of G major. Our first version here uses four fretted notes, making it fully moveable (see p. 72). For example, moving it up the neck by one fret results in the chord of Fm.

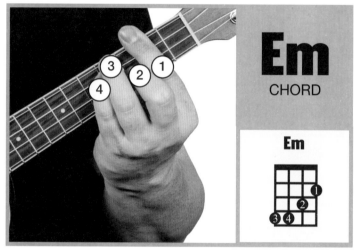

E MINOR ALT CHORD

If you find the full Em chord too challenging, try this easier shape using three fingers. The note G (the open G string) also belongs to the chord of Em, so it sounds fine, though because this is an open string the shape is not moveable.

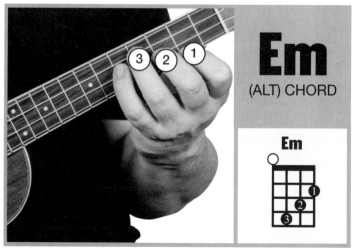

G MINOR CHORD

This chord is fairly easy to find. Note that although the fingering is different, only one note is actually changed compared with the G major chord. It is this note (known as the third of the chord) that decides whether a chord is major or minor. Try changing between G and G minor to hear this difference in quality.

Gm
CHORD

MODIFYING

Many simple chords in first position such as those we have learned so far can be modified by changing one note, and these changes can be used to decorate a ukulele strumming pattern. Try modifying any of the chords you have learned, for example by removing one finger and using the open string. The only rule is to listen to whether the result sounds good or not. For example, the Gm (or G) chord can be modified by adding the open A string. The resulting chord is called Gsus2.

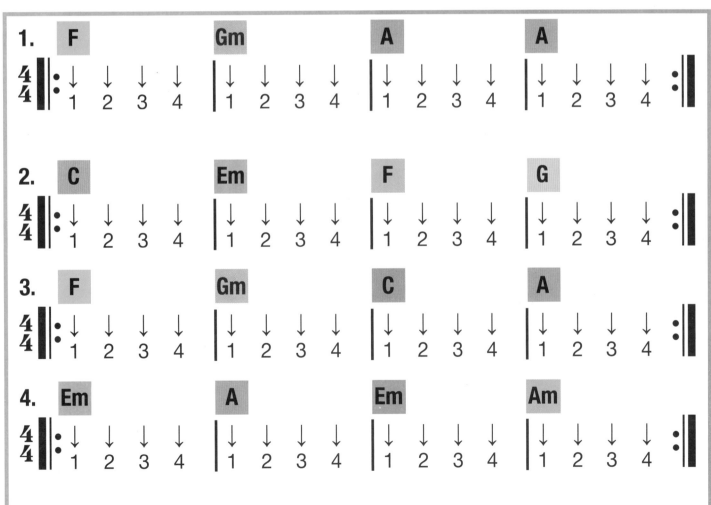

1. F Gm A A
2. C Em F G
3. F Gm C A
4. Em A Em Am

PLAY A SONG

Oh! Susanna

This classic song by Stephen Foster has been recorded by The Byrds and James Taylor. Our version in the key of C uses the chords C, Am, F and G.

CHORDS

VERSE

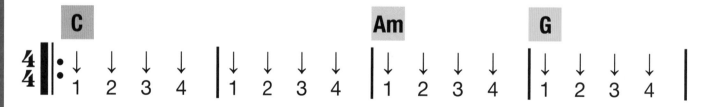

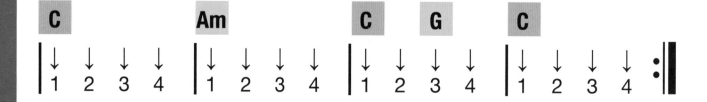

CHORUS

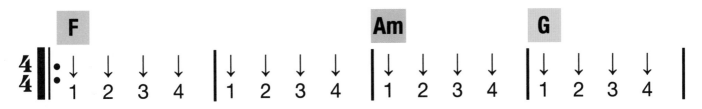

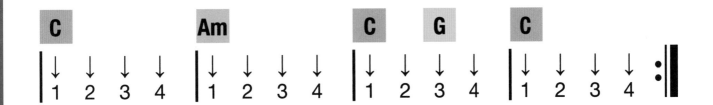

VERSE 1

| C | | | Am | | G | |
I come from Alabama with my banjo on my knee,

| C | | Am | | C | G | C |
I'm going to Louisiana my own true love for to see.

| C | | | Am | | G | |
It rained all night the day I left, the weather it was dry;

| C | | Am | | C | G | C |
The sun so hot I froze to death – Susanna don't you cry.

CHORUS

| F | | C | | G | |
Oh! Susanna don't you cry for me,

| C | | Am | | C | G | C |
I come from Alabama with my banjo on my knee.

VERSE 2

| C | | | Am | | G | |
I had a dream the other night when everything was still,

| C | | Am | | C | G | C |
I thought I saw Susanna dear, a-coming down the hill.

| C | | | Am | | G | |
A buckwheat cake was in her mouth; a tear was in her eye,

| C | | Am | | C | G | C |
I says I'se coming from the South – Susanna don't you cry.

Repeat Chorus

THE Dm CHORD

The Dm chord is like the F chord but with one extra fretted note. This makes it very easy to change between the two. This chord will enable you to play five-chord songs in the key of C, but it is also an important chord in other keys including F, A minor and D minor.

Dm
CHORD

UKULELE TIP: Try removing the first finger of the D minor chord. This creates an ambiguous chord called Dsus2.

Dm

This chord uses two fingers at the same fret on adjacent strings, as do many others. This can be tricky with large hands on a small (soprano) uke. As shown in the picture here, they will in reality be arranged more diagonally than the chord box suggests – just make sure they are both still within the fret area shown (between the first and second frets in this example).

CHORD CHANGING EXERCISES

1. F | Dm | F | C

$\frac{4}{4}$ ‖: ↓ ↓ ↓ ↓ | ↓ ↓ ↓ ↓ | ↓ ↓ ↓ ↓ | ↓ ↓ ↓ ↓ :‖
 1 2 3 4 | 1 2 3 4 | 1 2 3 4 | 1 2 3 4

2. Am | Dm | G | C

$\frac{4}{4}$ ‖: ↓ ↓ ↓ ↓ | ↓ ↓ ↓ ↓ | ↓ ↓ ↓ ↓ | ↓ ↓ ↓ ↓ :‖
 1 2 3 4 | 1 2 3 4 | 1 2 3 4 | 1 2 3 4

3. Dm | G | C | Am

$\frac{4}{4}$ ‖: ↓ ↓ ↓ ↓ | ↓ ↓ ↓ ↓ | ↓ ↓ ↓ ↓ | ↓ ↓ ↓ ↓ :‖
 1 2 3 4 | 1 2 3 4 | 1 2 3 4 | 1 2 3 4

4. C | Dm | F | G

$\frac{4}{4}$ ‖: ↓ ↓ ↓ ↓ | ↓ ↓ ↓ ↓ | ↓ ↓ ↓ ↓ | ↓ ↓ ↓ ↓ :‖
 1 2 3 4 | 1 2 3 4 | 1 2 3 4 | 1 2 3 4

5. Dm | Am | Dm | G

$\frac{4}{4}$ ‖: ↓ ↓ ↓ ↓ | ↓ ↓ ↓ ↓ | ↓ ↓ ↓ ↓ | ↓ ↓ ↓ ↓ :‖
 1 2 3 4 | 1 2 3 4 | 1 2 3 4 | 1 2 3 4

6. Dm | F | Dm | C

$\frac{4}{4}$ ‖: ↓ ↓ ↓ ↓ | ↓ ↓ ↓ ↓ | ↓ ↓ ↓ ↓ | ↓ ↓ ↓ ↓ :‖
 1 2 3 4 | 1 2 3 4 | 1 2 3 4 | 1 2 3 4

CHANGING STRINGS

Many professionals change their strings very often, but as a beginner you'll probably only want to do it a few times a year, or if one breaks. The exact procedure will depend on the design of your uke, but the principles are the same.

UKULELE TIP: Only use ukulele strings, and make sure they are the right gauge for your uke (soprano, concert, tenor, etc). NEVER use steel strings intended for guitar, mandolin or violin – these work at much higher tensions, which will probably do instant damage to the ukulele.

String Winder
A string winder will help you quickly get the string to approximately the right pitch.

String Trimmer
The string should be trimmed after being wound on in order to keep things tidy.

Even if you intend to change all four strings, to begin with you may want to change one at a time. This way, you can check that each new string is fitted in the same way as the others before you move on.

EQUIPMENT
A string winder and trimmer can be used for removing old strings, trimming new ones and quickly winding the new string to approximately the right tension.

REMOVING THE OLD STRING
Slacken the string completely, and then cut it anywhere between the bridge and the nut. Disentangle both ends of the string. Take this opportunity to remove any dust or grime exposed by removing the string.

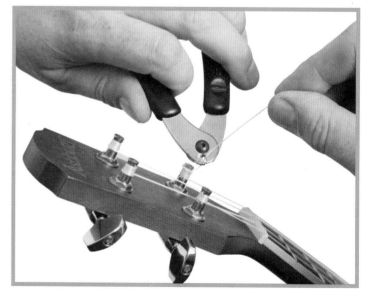

ATTACHING THE NEW STRING AT THE BRIDGE

There are two main types of bridge, designed for different kinds of strings; some bridges will accommodate both types. Ball end strings are the easiest to fit, as they simply pass through the bridge and anchor automatically. Plain end strings need to be tied to the bridge, much like classical guitar strings. The process is quite hard to describe; the best idea is to inspect the old strings to make sure you understand how they are fitted. Essentially, the string is fended through the bridge the 'wrong' way, looped back under itself, and then twisted around itself several times on the surface of the bridge.

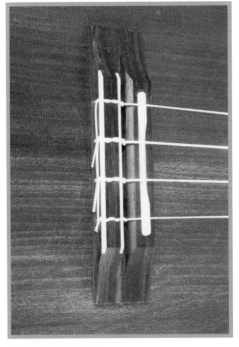

Attaching the string to the bridge
Attaching the string to a classical guitar-style bridge. This should be tight before attaching the other end.

Trimming
To achieve a tidy result like this, the strings may need to be trimmed after attaching to the bridge (right).

ATTACHING TO THE TUNING PEG

The string should be fed through the tuning peg/machine head and looped around itself so that the string will be held in place by its own tension. There should be enough slack to allow the string to be wound around the tuning peg at least four or five times.

Attaching the string to the tuning peg
Right and below: First the string is looped through the machine head before pulling the string tight and winding it on.

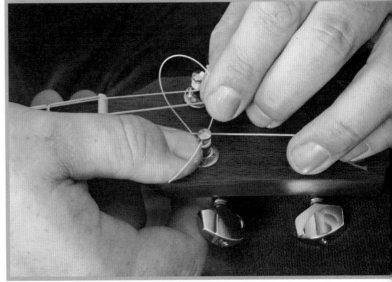

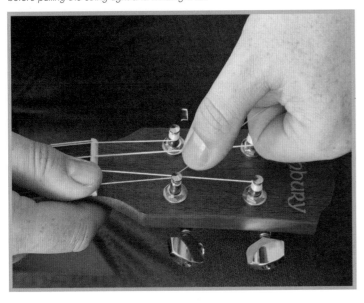

TUNING NEW STRINGS

Uke strings are made of soft nylon. This takes a while to stretch, so new uke strings may need a lot of re-tuning before they stabilize. You can speed up this process a little by tuning to the correct pitch, giving the string a sharp upwards tug, and then repeating the process. Each tug will lower the pitch of the string, but this should become less pronounced each time.

PLAY A SONG

The Water Is Wide

This classic Scottish ballad has been recorded by many artists including James Taylor and Eva Cassidy. This song uses six of the eight chords we have learned so far. Take this at a steady tempo in order to fit in the quick changes on beat 4.

CHORD SEQUENCE

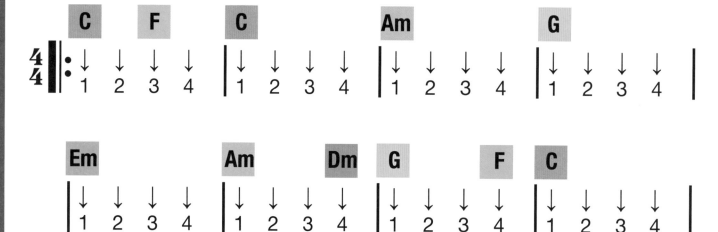

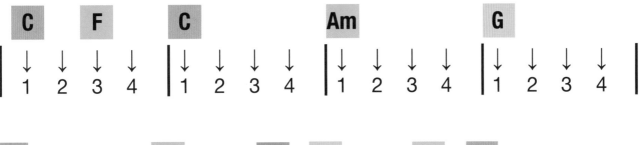

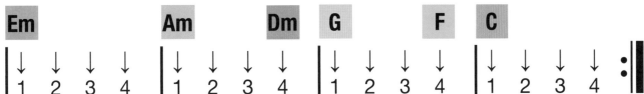

VERSE 1

C **F**   **C**
The water is wide,   I can't get o'er.

          Am   **G**
And neither have I the wings to fly.

          Em   **Am**
Build me a boat that can carry two,

Dm   **G**   **F**   **C**
And both shall row, my love and I.

VERSE 2

C **F**   **C**
There is a ship   and she sails the seas,

          Am   **G**
She's loaded deep, as deep can be;

          Em   **Am**
But not as deep as the love I'm in,

Dm   **G**   **F**   **C**
I know not how I sink or swim.

VERSE 3

C **F**   **C**
I leaned my back   'gainst a young oak,

          Am   **G**
Thinking he was a trusty tree.

          Em   **Am**
But first he bent and then he broke,

Dm **G**   **F**   **C**
And so did my false love to me.

VERSE 4

C   **F**   **C**
O love is handsome   and love is fine,

          Am   **G**
And love's a jewel while it's first new.

          Em   **Am**
But love grows old and waxes cold

Dm **G**   **F**   **C**
And fades away like morning dew.

UKULELE HEROES

UKULELE ORCHESTRA OF GREAT BRITAIN

1985–

RECOMMENDED LISTENING:
Anarchy In The UK (DVD)
"Shaft"
"Teenage Dirtbag"

The Ukulele Orchestra of Great Britain was formed in 1985 in order to 'challenge people's expectation of the ukulele'. Since then, the UOGB has become something of a national institution in Britain, with regular performances on TV, radio and major music festivals including Glastonbury and The Proms.

UOGB's line-up has varied since 1985 but in recent years it has settled into the format of an octet, including one bass ukulele. Several members of the group also sing both lead and backing vocals.

The orchestra's repertoire spans a wide range of styles from classical arrangements and film themes to pop, rock and even punk songs, with frequent use of unexpected stylistic juxtapositions (for example, the Sex Pistols' "Anarchy in the UK" performed in the style of Simon & Garfunkel, and Kate Bush's "Wuthering Heights" as a jazz number).

The Ukulele Orchestra has released more than a dozen albums and several concert DVDs during its career. It has also worked on collaborations including founder George Hinchliffe's opera "Dreamspiel", and the Ukulelescope project, in which the orchestra provides live musical accompaniment to silent films. UOGB concerts often include an element of audience participation. In 2009, they performed at a Prom concert at London's Royal Albert Hall. During the performance nearly 1000 audience members joined in for a performance of Beethoven's "Ode To Joy", setting a world record for the number of uke players performing simultaneously.

FAVOURED INSTRUMENTS:

VARIOUS

Touring in Berlin, Germany
Ukulele Orchestra of 2012 line-up, with the greater part of the ukulele family.

CHAPTER 3:
EXPLORING RHYTHMS

In this chapter we will add rhythmic detail and fluidity by strumming upwards as well as downwards.

LEFT: Kris Fuchigami is known as being an engaging performer with lightning fast hands.

UPSTROKES

So far, we have been strumming in one direction only: downwards. Since the hand has to move upwards between each downstroke, this upward motion can also be used to play the strings. Whether using the fingers or a pick, these strokes are called upstrokes.

Upstroke: The right hand strums the strings during its upward motion between beats.

PREPARATION – COUNTING OFFBEATS

Strums or notes occurring between beats are called offbeats. To understand these, start by counting '1, 2, 3, 4' in time with a metronome or other regular pulse. Next, add an 'and' between beats:

'**1** & 2 & 3 & 4 & **1** & 2 & 3 & 4 &'

The offbeats should fall exactly halfway between the beats. Once this seems natural, do the same thing on the ukulele. Start by strumming any chord on every beat, then add upstrokes for the offbeats.

MIXED PATTERNS

Strumming patterns often include some, but not all, of the offbeats. If we are using upstrokes for the offbeats, this should remain consistent, and downstrokes should always be used on the beat. Missing out some of the offbeats will therefore still involve performing an upstroke, but one where you miss the strings rather than playing them. This is called a phantom or ghost stroke.

Practise the following strumming patterns, remembering that downstrokes should always fall on the beat, and upstrokes should be on the offbeat – whether they are heard or phantom strokes.

REGGAE

The reggae style can work surprisingly well on ukulele as it can take on the role of the rhythm guitar, which usually plays fairly high chord voicings. In this style, rhythm parts often use upstrokes (on the offbeat) almost exclusively. For this to make sense something has to be playing (or singing) on the beat, however.

EXERCISES

These exercises combine all of the chords learned so far with many possible rhythms using downstrokes and upstrokes. For now at least, downstrokes should always be used on the beat, and upstrokes on the offbeat. To help you maintain focus on changing chords, the strumming rhythm will be the same for the duration of each exercise.

BUILDING A CHORD

The shapes we have learned so far form the basis of many simple accompaniments, but it can also be useful to be able to construct chords yourself. If you know the names of all the notes on the first four frets, and the notes needed to build a range of chords, you can try finding chords yourself.

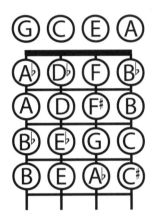

The diagram above shows all the notes in the first four frets. The notes A, B, C, D, E, F and G are called natural notes – these are the white notes on a piano. The notes in between, or black notes, are called sharps and flats. Each of these actually has two possible names; we have shown the commonest name for each for the sake of simplicity.

However, you will also need to know the alternative names:

$F\sharp$ (F sharp) = $G\flat$ (G flat)

$A\flat$ (A flat) = $G\sharp$ (G sharp)

$B\flat$ (B flat) = $A\sharp$ (A sharp)

$C\sharp$ (C sharp) = $D\flat$ (D flat)

$E\flat$ (E flat) = $D\sharp$ (D sharp)

CHORD SPELLINGS

To make a major or minor chord, three different notes need to appear at least once: the root (which gives the chord its name), third and fifth. As the ukulele has four strings, either one string will not be played or (usually) all four strings will be played and one note will be 'doubled' (appear twice). For now, this can be any note in the chord.

	Major			Minor		
	Root	Third	Fifth	Root	Third	Fifth
C	C	E	G	C	$E\flat$	G
D	D	$F\sharp$	A	D	F	A
E	E	$G\sharp$	B	E	G	B
F	F	A	C	F	$A\flat$	C
G	G	B	D	G	$B\flat$	D
A	A	$C\sharp$	E	A	C	E
B	B	$D\sharp$	$F\sharp$	B	D	$F\sharp$

PLAY A SONG

The Raggle Taggle Gypsy

This folk ballad is often played at a rousing fast tempo. You may need to start at a slower pace. Try to get the strumming pattern as smooth as possible, and don't be afraid to vary it. If you like, you can play just beats 1, 2 and 3 (using downstrokes) in the final bar to emphasize the words.

CHORDS

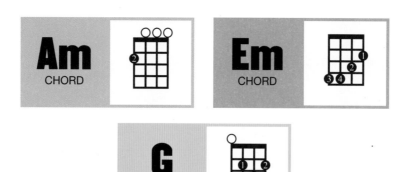

CHORD SEQUENCE

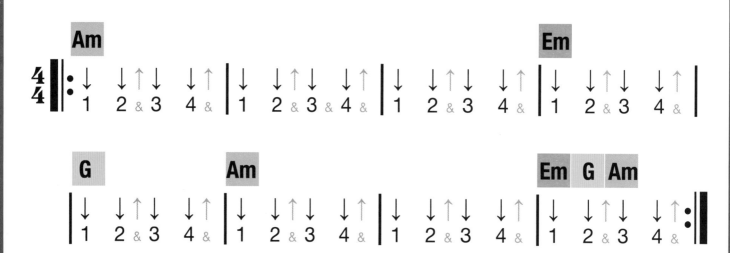

VERSE 1

Am

There were three old gypsies came to our hall door,

Em

They came brave and boldly-o.

G   Am

And one sang high and the other sang low,

Em G Am

And the other sang a raggle taggle gyp – sy-o

VERSE 2

Am

It was late that night when the Lord came in,

Em

Enquiring for his lady-o.

G   Am

And the servant girl she said to the Lord,

Em G Am

'She's away wi' the raggle taggle gyp – sy-o.'

VERSE 3

Am

Now he rode East and he rode West,

Em

He rode North and South also.

G   Am

Until he came to a wide open plain,

Em G Am

It was there that he spied his la – dy-o.

VERSE 4

Am

'How could you leave your house and your land?

Em

How could you leave your money-o?

G   Am

How could you leave your only wedded Lord,

Em G Am

All for a raggle taggle gyp – sy - o?'

VERSE 5

Am

'What care I for my house and my land?,

Em

What care I for my money-o?

G   Am

I'd rather have a kiss from the yellow gypsy's lips,

Em G Am

I'm away wi' the raggle taggle gyp – sy-o!'

UKULELE IKE

1895–1971

RECOMMENDED LISTENING:
"It's Only A Paper Moon"
"Singin' In The Rain"
"I Can't Give You Anything But Love"

Cliff Edwards, usually known as Ukulele Ike, was an American singer, ukulele player and entertainer. In a career spanning more than 50 years, he had many hits, performed in a large number of films and played a key role in the popularization of the ukulele.

Edwards was one of the most successful recording artists of the 1920s, recording many jazzy versions of the standards of the time, including one of the earliest recordings of scat singing. He appeared alongside Fred Astaire in George and Ira Gershwin's first Broadway musical "Lady Be Good". He had many top ten hits during the 1920s, including "Singin' In The Rain", "I Can't Give You Anything But Love"

and many of his own compositions. The ukulele became a hugely popular instrument at this time, with millions sold, and publishers adding ukulele chord boxes to sheet music.

During the 1930s, Edwards transitioned into the new medium of talking pictures, with dozens of roles in the first few years of the format. While some of these were pure acting roles, others featured Edwards singing and playing his ukulele, including a brief appearance alongside Joan Crawford.

Edwards' popularity as a singer waned as his Vaudeville-inspired singing style (often with high, exuberant scat singing) gave way to the 'crooner' style of Bing Crosby and, later, Frank

Sinatra. Edwards retained a career in film, mainly as a voiceover artist, appearing in Disney's animated films. It was in this guise that he recorded one of his biggest hits, the Oscar-winning "When You Wish Upon A Star" (from "Pinocchio", in which he voiced the character Jiminy Cricket).

Uke Fame
Like George Formby in Britain, Ukulele Ike popularized the ukulele in America. Sadly, in spite of his fame, he died in poverty.

FAVOURED INSTRUMENT:

**MARTIN SOPRANO
(LATER TENOR)**

CHAPTER 4:

GETTING BLUESY

Most popular music is in some way derived from or influenced by the blues. The most obvious effect of the blues on other music is its use of 'seventh' chords rather than just simple major and minor chords.

SEVENTH CHORDS

So far we have used two types of chord: major and minor. These are the simplest chords found in most music, as they contain just three unique notes. Seventh chords add a fourth unique note and therefore sound more complex. They are often found in blues and derived styles including jazz and rock.

Many seventh chords can be constructed by changing just one note in a triad shape. Although they may use up to all four fingers, most seventh chords in 'friendly' keys on the uke contain some open strings. The E7 chord shown here contains one open string. Because this open string is an 'inside' string, there is a greater chance that you will mute it accidentally. If the chord does not sound clearly, pick the strings one at a time to check which one is not sounding. If one of your fingers is accidentally muting the open string, you will probably feel it in this finger when picking the string, and you'll be able to correct the problem.

E7
CHORD

E7

LISTEN

There is something about the quality of a seventh chord that seems to make it 'want' to move to a certain chord. Listen to the sequences opposite as you play the exercises, and notice how E7 to Am sounds expected, whereas Am to another chord such as F or D sounds like a surprise.

EXERCISES

Chord charts are often written without specific rhythms. 'Real world' chord charts often show just the time signature barlines, with four slashes (if we are in **4/4**) to represent the beats in each bar. The exact rhythms used, and other stylistic issues, are decided by the individual musician.

For these exercises, try to make up your own rhythms or use ones from previous exercises. As before, maintain one rhythm for the whole exercise; this will help you maintain focus on the changing chords in time. If you are finding this challenging, you can let each chord ring for a whole bar, before progressing to two strums per chord, then one strum, and finally more developed rhythms using upstrokes. Turn the page for more seventh chords.

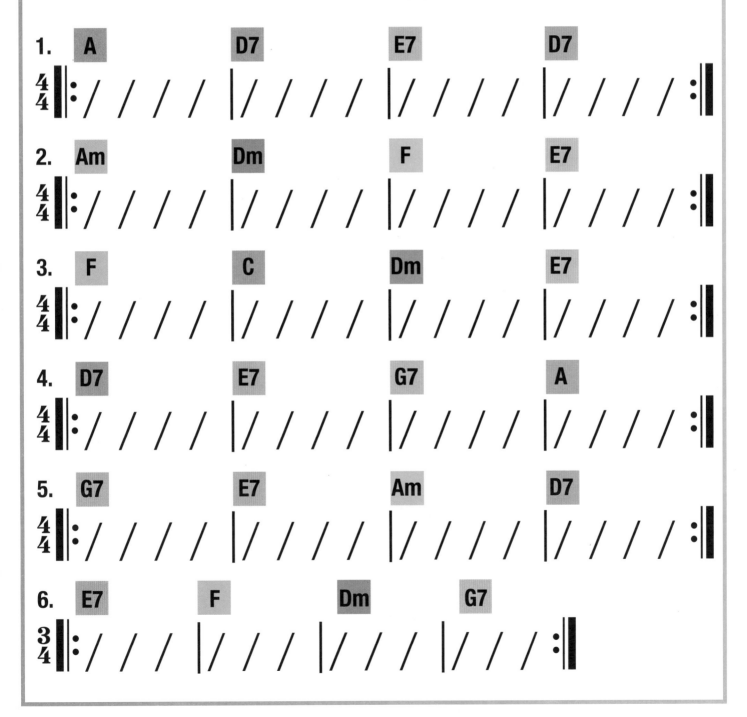

MORE SEVENTH CHORDS

Any major chord can be turned into a seventh chord. This usually involves changing just one note, so seventh chords can be easy to remember, though this sometimes results in fretting the notes with different fingers. The most common seventh chords are shown by simply adding '7' after the name of the root note.

In the A7 and D7 shapes below, the change is very simple: one fretted note is removed; the extra note is an open string. For A7, the rest of the fingers are unaffected; you could take this approach to D7 too, but most players use fingers 2 and 3 as this is a bit more comfortable.

For the G7 chord, the seventh is a fretted note, which means that different fingers have to be used to play the other notes.

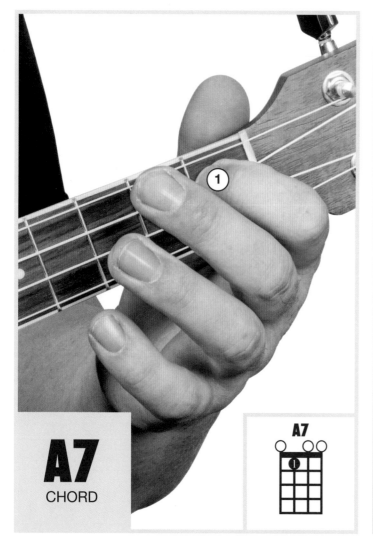

A7 CHORD

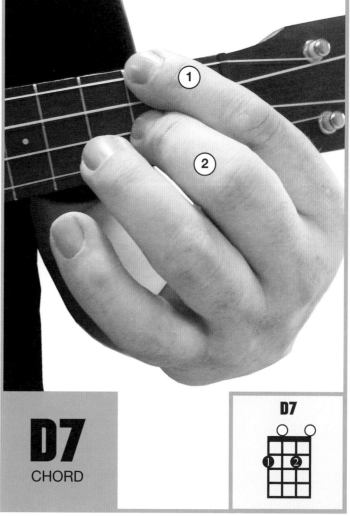

D7 CHORD

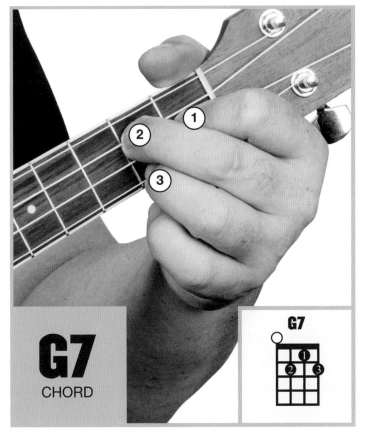

G7 CHORD

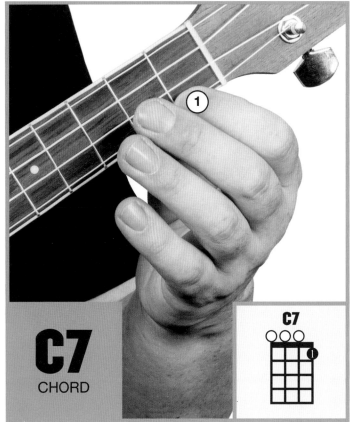

C7 CHORD

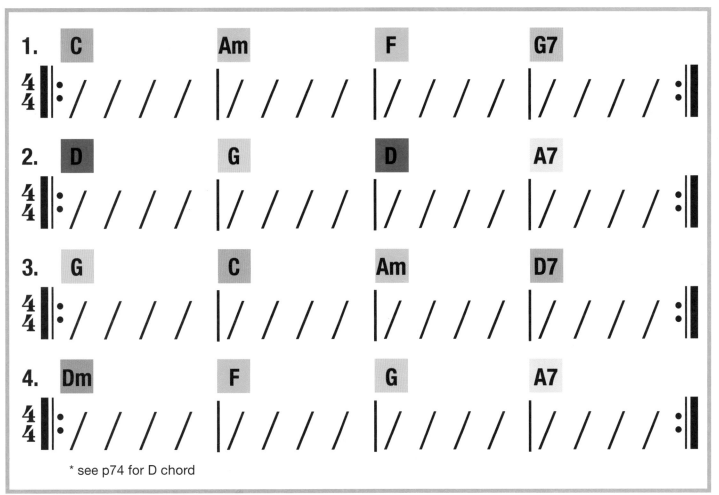

1. C   Am   F   G7

2. D   G   D   A7

3. G   C   Am   D7

4. Dm   F   G   A7

* see p74 for D chord

THE TWELVE BAR BLUES

The origins of this three-chord song structure are lost in the mists of time; it is likely that it originated at least 150 years ago. It is probably the most commonly used chord sequence in history, certainly in a lot of popular music. Possibly because so many songs use this sequence, it always feels completely 'right' – and not just for songs that start with 'I woke up this morning...'.

As its name suggests, this twelve-bar sequence is central to the music known as the blues, but has also formed the basis of a substantial proportion of rock, pop and jazz – in the latter case, often in more advanced versions employing far more than three chords.

In its basic form, the twelve-bar sequence is found in hundreds of blues and rock 'n' roll classics. Once you have the measure of the sequence, you can try any of these songs yourself. Seventh chords have a fundamentally 'bluesy' character, but for some styles simpler major chords are used. In the exercise below you can play A anywhere you see A7, for example.

TRY THESE BLUES SONGS...

If you know any of these songs, try singing them along to the twelve-bar sequence below: they will all work ...

"Kansas City"   "Twenty Flight Rock"
"Sweet Home Chicago"   "Johnny B. Goode"

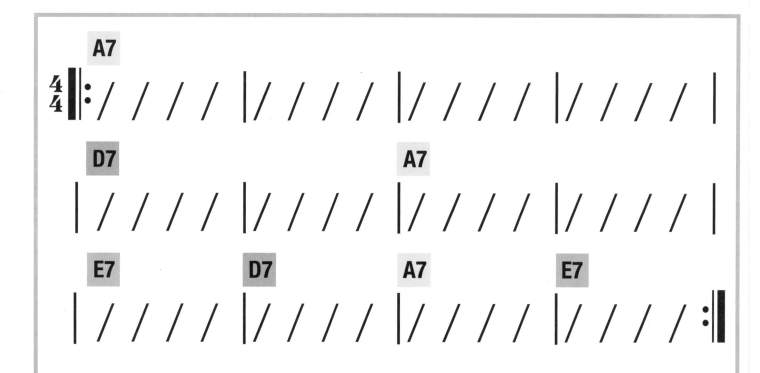

RAGTIME

This musical style originated on the piano but lends itself to the ukulele. Some players such as James Hill (see pp. 78–79) have developed a playing style incorporating melody and chords. Ragtime chord sequences are often highly satisfying to play on their own, and they also make great practice.

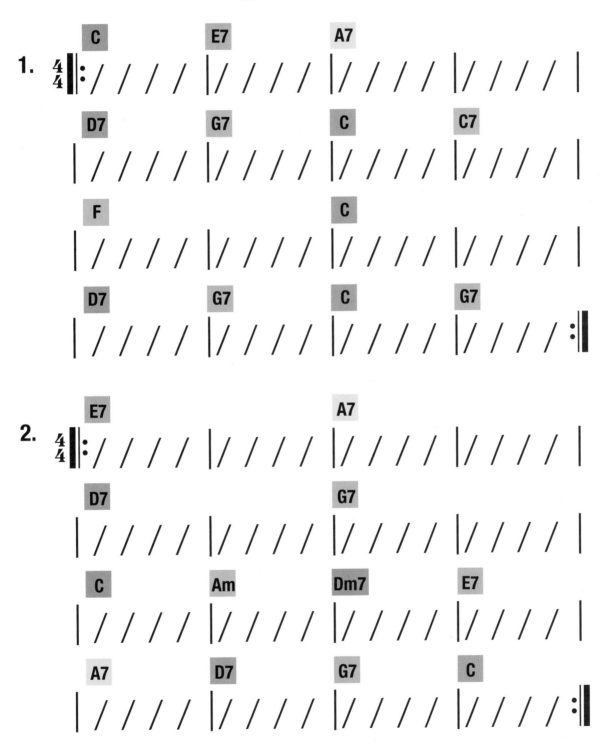

RAGTIME SEQUENCES

PLAY A SONG

Blame It On The Blues

This song by Ma Rainey comes from the dawn of the blues. If the key does not suit your voice, you could try transposing it into a different key using other seventh chords. The sequence here is in the key of D, but you could try it in A (A7, D7, E7) or C (C7, F7, G7).

CHORDS

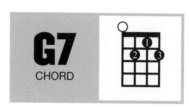

CHORD SEQUENCE

D7

$\frac{4}{4}$ ‖: / / / / | / / / / | / / / / | / / / / |

G7   D7

| / / / / | / / / / | / / / / | / / / / |

A7   G7   D7   A7

| / / / / | / / / / | / / / / | / / / / :‖

VERSE 1

`D7`
I'm so sad and worried, got no time to spread the news,

`G7`   `D7`
I'm so sad and worried, got no time to spread the news.

    `A7`   `G7`   `D7`
Won't blame it on my troubles, can't blame it on the blues.

VERSE 2

`D7`
I can't blame my daddy, he treats me nice and kind,

`G7`   `D7`
I can't blame my daddy, he treats me nice and kind.

    `A7`   `G7`   `D7`   `A7`
Shall I blame it on my nephew, blame it on that trouble of mine?

VERSE 3

    `D7`
This house is like a graveyard when I'm left here by myself,

      `G7`   `D7`
This house is like a graveyard when I'm left here by myself,

      `A7`   `G7`   `D7`   `A7`
Shall I blame it on my lover? Blame it on somebody else.

VERSE 4

`D7`
  Can't blame it on my mother, can't blame my dad,

  Can't blame my brother for the trouble I've had.

`G7`
  Can't blame my lover, that held my hand,

`D7`
  Can't blame my husband, can't blame my man.

`A7`   `G7`   `D7`   `A7`
  Can't blame nobody, guess I'll have to blame it on the blues.

USING A CAPO

The capo is a handy device that makes it possible to play in different keys without learning new chord shapes, by effectively shortening the ukulele's scale length and strings by fixing it to the neck. There are many different types of capo; most use either some form of spring tension or elastic to stay in place and push the strings down.

If you are playing with other musicians and using a capo to transpose (move up or down to another key) the key of a song, some knowledge of music theory may be needed in order to work out what key you end up with. At this stage, you can at least tell them where you have placed the capo. One fret corresponds to a semitone (the smallest interval in music), and two frets is a tone (two semitones), so if you are using a capo at the second fret you can say that you have transposed up a tone.

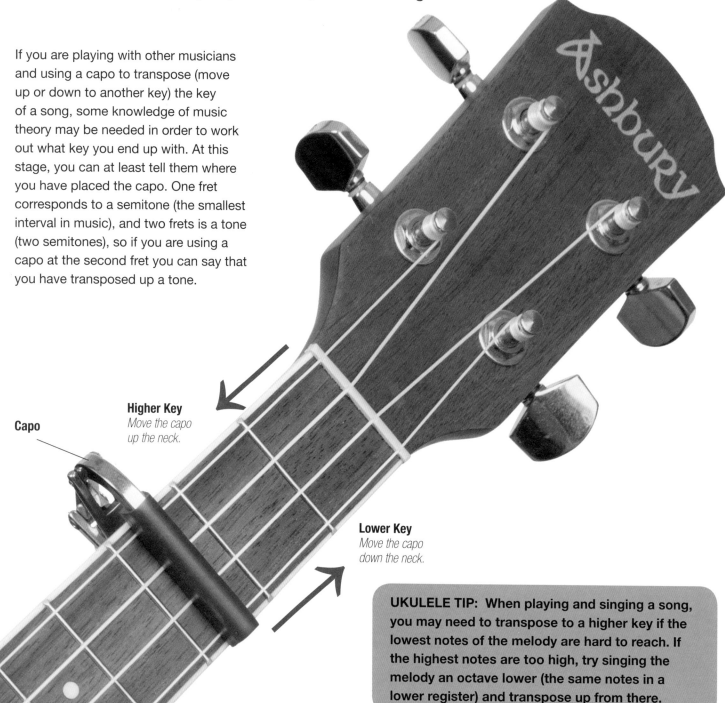

Capo

Higher Key
Move the capo up the neck.

Lower Key
Move the capo down the neck.

UKULELE TIP: When playing and singing a song, you may need to transpose to a higher key if the lowest notes of the melody are hard to reach. If the highest notes are too high, try singing the melody an octave lower (the same notes in a lower register) and transpose up from there.

CHOOSING A CAPO

When buying a capo, make sure you buy a dedicated ukulele capo and not a guitar one. Although some guitar capos may just about stay in place on a ukulele, they are really too big, at least for the smaller members of the uke family. Not all music stores carry these but they are readily available to buy online. Make sure the model you order is suitable for your particular uke size.

THE RIGHT FIT

Some guitar capos are designed for fretboards that are not completely flat, so they are slightly curved. These may not work well on the uke's flat fretboard.

C-clamp Capo

Elastic Capo

CHAPTER 5:

BARRE CHORDS

These chords, unlike chords with open strings, can be moved up and down the fretboard, giving access to the whole range of keys on the ukulele.

LEFT: American singer-songwriter Meghan Trainor plays a variety of musical instruments: ukulele, bass, guitar, keyboard, trumpet, percussion and piano.

BARRE CHORDS

As the uke has four strings and the left hand has four fingers, in theory any conceivable chord shape can be played within a reasonable range of frets. However, there are many chords where several notes are used at the same fret. Cramming two or more fingers this close together would be impossible for most players. The simple solution is to use the side of one finger to fret several strings at once. Chords constructed in this way are called barre chords.

WHAT IS A BARRE?

A full barre with the first finger (across all four strings) can be viewed almost like a capo as it raises the pitch of all four strings together. We then have three fingers left to construct any chord shape, which will be transposed accordingly. Barre chords on the guitar are crucial to many players as the guitar has six strings but they only have four fingers. On the uke they are still important but much less challenging.

B♭
CHORD

B♭m
CHORD

One of the most useful barre chord shapes is based on the A shape (p. 36). Transposing this up by one semitone (using a barre at the first fret) gives us a B♭ (B flat) chord.

Removing the second finger from the B♭ chord changes its quality from major to minor, resulting in a B♭m (B flat minor) chord.

Barre chords can be tough for a beginner to master, though they are much easier on the ukulele than the guitar. Using barre chords for a whole song can cause some strain, but you don't always have to – mixing them with easier chords can open up many keys and sequences that would otherwise be impossible, as explored in the exercises below.

EXERCISES

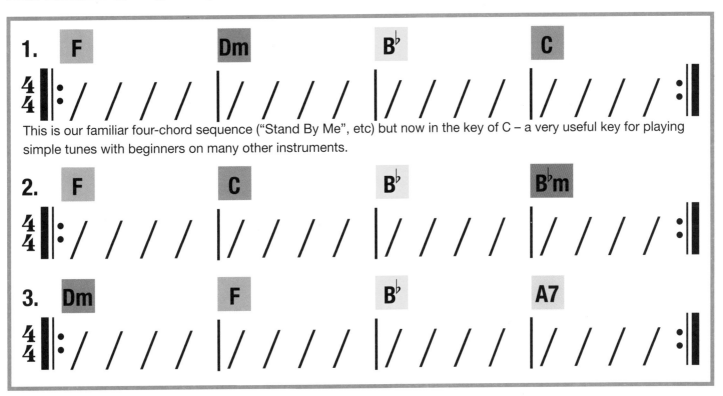

1.   F   Dm   B♭   C

This is our familiar four-chord sequence ("Stand By Me", etc) but now in the key of C – a very useful key for playing simple tunes with beginners on many other instruments.

2.   F   C   B♭   B♭m

3.   Dm   F   B♭   A7

MORE BARRE CHORDS

Many other shapes can be transposed using the barre technique. The C shape is very easy to move – most players do this using an index finger barre plus the fourth finger. This is shown here at the second fret, resulting in an alternative D chord shape. The F shape is also easy to move, as shown here at the third fret, resulting in an A♭ chord.

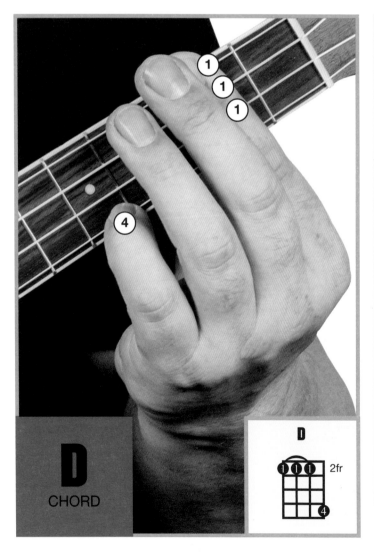

D
CHORD

D
2fr

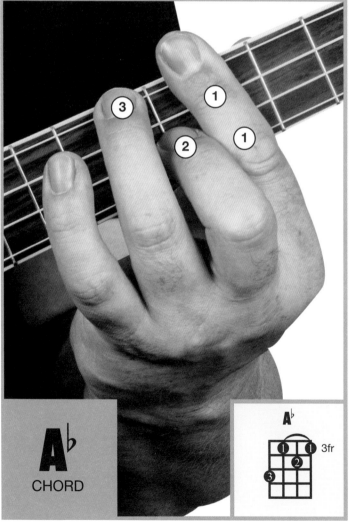

A♭
CHORD

A♭
3fr

UKULELE TIP: If you have come to the ukulele from the guitar, you may be used to the idea of chords with the root note as the lowest (bass) note. This is much less important on the uke, partly because of its higher range (so there are no real bass notes anyway) and partly because of its re-entrant tuning complicating matters. So don't worry about it!

UKULELE TIP: Any uke chord containing four fretted notes can be moved up and down the fretboard – it doesn't have to be a barre chord. Chords containing open strings can sometimes be moved around too – either avoid playing the open strings, or try playing them anyway – the results can sometimes be interesting.

EXERCISES

These exercises combine familiar chords with barre shapes. Use the D barre shape for D. The Bm chord is exactly the same B♭m, just one fret higher.

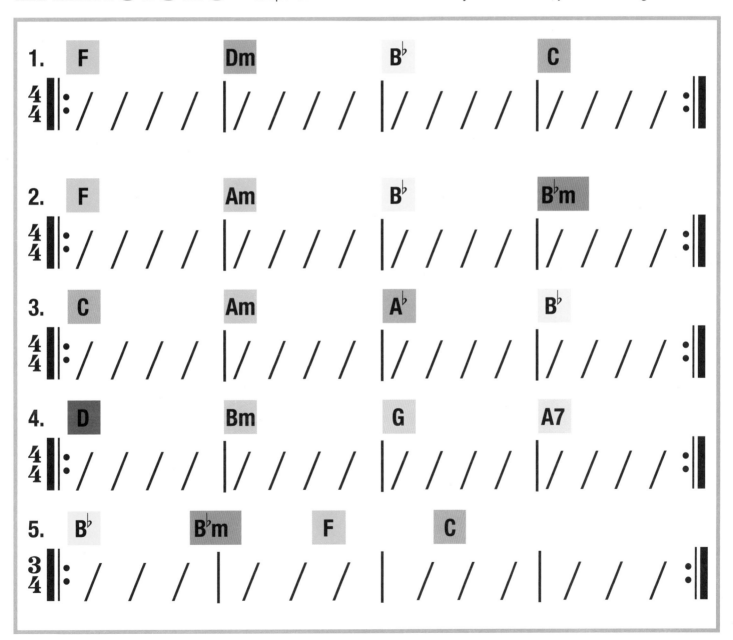

Aura Lea

This song from the American Civil War achieved greater fame with different lyrics as Elvis Presley's "Love Me Tender". In the key of F, we can use both the B♭ and B♭m barre chords. Keep the strumming simple, but you can introduce a few upstrokes for variety.

CHORDS

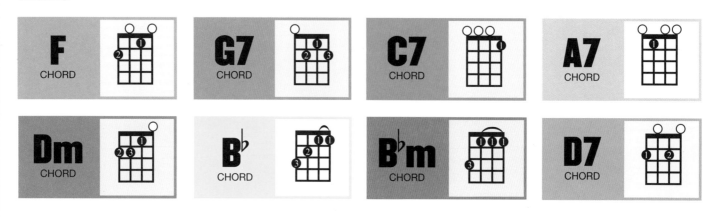

CHORD SEQUENCE

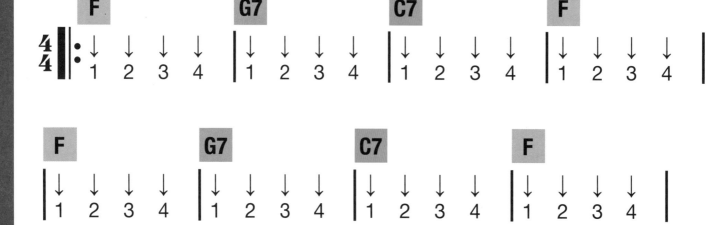

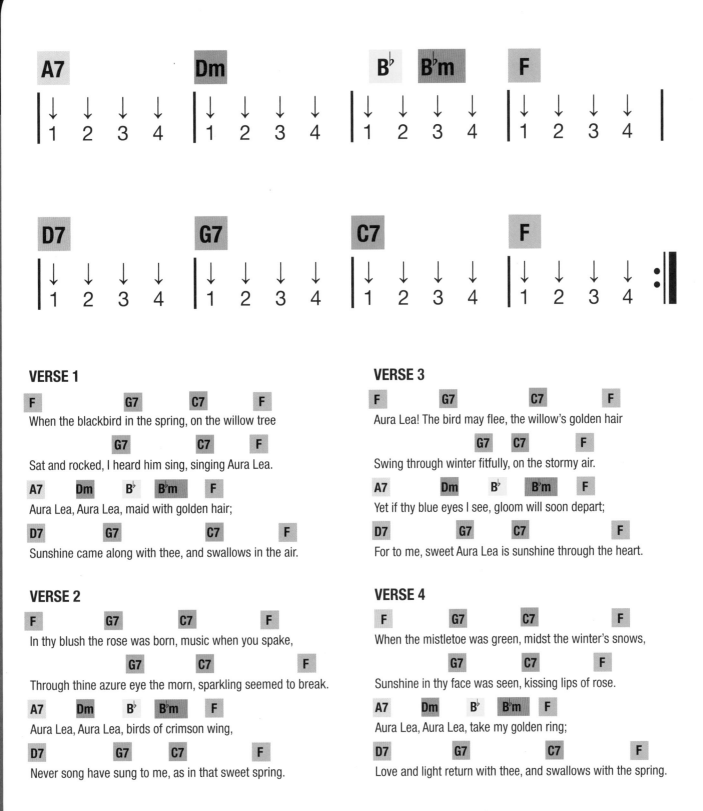

VERSE 1

F		G7		C7		F

When the blackbird in the spring, on the willow tree

		G7		C7		F

Sat and rocked, I heard him sing, singing Aura Lea.

A7	Dm	B♭	B♭m	F

Aura Lea, Aura Lea, maid with golden hair;

D7	G7		C7		F

Sunshine came along with thee, and swallows in the air.

VERSE 2

F		G7		C7		F

In thy blush the rose was born, music when you spake,

		G7		C7		F

Through thine azure eye the morn, sparkling seemed to break.

A7	Dm	B♭	B♭m	F

Aura Lea, Aura Lea, birds of crimson wing,

D7		G7		C7		F

Never song have sung to me, as in that sweet spring.

VERSE 3

F		G7		C7		F

Aura Lea! The bird may flee, the willow's golden hair

		G7	C7		F

Swing through winter fitfully, on the stormy air.

A7	Dm	B♭	B♭m	F

Yet if thy blue eyes I see, gloom will soon depart;

D7		G7		C7		F

For to me, sweet Aura Lea is sunshine through the heart.

VERSE 4

F		G7		C7		F

When the mistletoe was green, midst the winter's snows,

		G7		C7		F

Sunshine in thy face was seen, kissing lips of rose.

A7	Dm	B♭	B♭m	F

Aura Lea, Aura Lea, take my golden ring;

D7		G7		C7		F

Love and light return with thee, and swallows with the spring.

UKULELE HEROES

JAMES HILL
1980–

RECOMMENDED LISTENING:
"Uke Talk"
"Indecision Rag"
"One Small Suite for Ukulele"

James Hill is a Canadian virtuoso ukulele player, composer and educator. The ukulele has been a popular instrument in Canada since the 1970s, when it began to be used in schools as a result of the work of J. Chalmers Doane and his book *Ukulele in the Classroom*. James Hill participated in the Langley Ukulele Ensemble (a direct spinoff from Doane's activities) for many years before embarking on a solo career.

Hill has recorded many albums, including both original compositions and covers of songs such as Jimi Hendrix's "Little Wing". He is also a fine singer; many of his recordings fall squarely into the North American folk tradition, though with an added twist on some recordings supplied by his partner, the classically trained cellist Anne Janelle (previously Anne Davidson). Their award-winning album *True Love Don't Weep* (2009) features ukulele, cello and vocals from both of them.

James Hill's music spans many styles including bluegrass, ragtime, classical and pop. His playing style combines elements of classical guitar technique with ideas more reminiscent of banjo and melodic jazz guitar. His solo performances often combine melody, chords and percussive elements seamlessly. His concerts are generally accompanied by workshops, and both are thoroughly entertaining and involving. He has toured internationally.

In 2008 Hill collaborated with J. Chalmers Doane to produce a classroom ukulele method for the next generation: *Ukulele in the Classroom – James Hill Ukulele Method*.

Promoting the uke
James Hill has made a massive contribution to the ukulele's recent popular resurgence.

FAVOURED
INSTRUMENT:

**MIKE DASILVA
CUSTOM**

SYNCOPATION

Just as we can miss the strings to produce a phantom upstroke, the same idea can be used to give phantom downstrokes. This results in a greater emphasis on the offbeats (upstrokes) – a musical effect known as syncopation.

To produce one of the most useful syncopated strumming patterns, start with this rhythm:

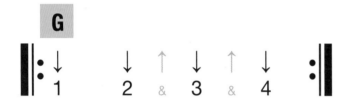

For the full syncopated effect, beat 2 here should be played lightly, and the offbeat between 2 and 3 should be emphasized. In fact, you can create an even more syncopated rhythm by also putting a phantom downstroke on beat 2…

Now simply omit the downstroke on beat 3, making sure that you still perform a 'phantom' downstroke instead (shown here in brackets).

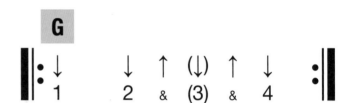

…and even placing an extra upstroke between 1 and 2:

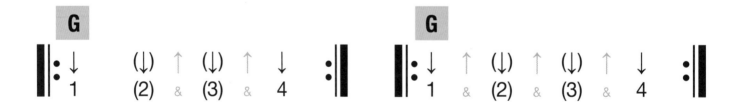

To play these rhythms fluently, it is vital to stick to the rule: downstrokes on the beat, upstrokes on the offbeat. This basic rule works for many styles, though for some the rate has to be double so there are four strokes per beat (down, up, down, up). For these exercises, tap your foot on the beat and imagine it is attached with string to your picking hand.

ON THE BEAT

Syncopation only works if the listener can identify where the beat is. If you are playing with a band where the bass and drums are playing mainly on the beat, you can play offbeats exclusively; some styles such as reggae and ska make heavy use of this idea. If you are playing on your own you will need to play on the beat at least once per bar, usually on beat 1 – otherwise all your upstrokes will sound like beats rather than offbeats.

SYNCOPATED SONGS

These well-known songs use syncopated strumming patterns or riffs:

- Oasis: "Wonderwall"
- George Harrison: "My Sweet Lord"
- Van Morrison: "Brown Eyed Girl"
- Elvis Presley: "His Latest Flame"
- Kings Of Leon: "Use Somebody"

PRACTICE SEQUENCES

Try applying any of the three rhythms shown above to these chord sequences.

1. Am | D7 | Am | G

2. Dm | B♭ | F | C

3. C | F | D7 | G7

4. G | G7 | C | Am

PLAY A SONG

Wade In The Water

This song should be played using a swing feel. This means that the off-beats, instead of falling exactly in between the beats, should be played later. This rhythm is the basis of a lot of jazz and blues, and many songs in other styles too. The easiest way to understand it is to listen to some examples:

- Any recording of this song
- Nina Simone: "Work Song"
- Duke Ellington: "C Jam Blues"

CHORDS

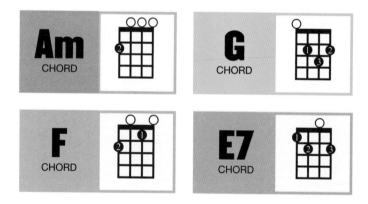

STRUMMING PATTERN/INTRO

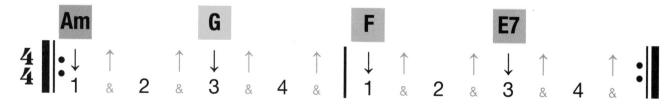

UKULELE TIP: For a more bluesy feel, you could turn the G and F chords into 7 chords too. The shapes are easy and can be found in the Chord Reference section.

VERSE 1

`Am`　　`G`　　`F`　　`E7`
Who's that young girl dressed in red?

`Am`　`G`　`F`　`E7`
Wade　in the wa - ter,

`Am`　　`G`　　`F`　`E7`
Must be the children that Moses led.

`Am*`　`(N.C.)`　　`E7`
God's gonna trouble the water.

VERSE 2

`Am`　　`G`　　`F`　　`E7`
Who's that young girl dressed in white?

`Am`　`G`　`F`　`E7`
Wade　in the wa - ter,

`Am`　　`G`　　`F`　`E7`
Must be the children of Isra - el.

`Am*`　`(N.C.)`　　`E7`
God's gonna trouble the water.

VERSE 3

`Am`　　`G`　　`F`　　`E7`
Who's that young girl dressed in blue?

`Am`　`G`　`F`　`E7`
Wade　in the wa - ter,

`Am`　　`G`　　`F`　`E7`
Must be the children that's coming true.

`Am*`　`(N.C.)`　　`E7`
God's gonna trouble the water.

CHORUS (REPEAT BETWEEN VERSES)

`Am`　`G`　`F`　`E7`
Wade　in the wa - ter,

`Am`　`G`　`F`　`E7`
Wade　in the water children.

`Am`　　`G`　`F`　`E7`
Wade　in the wa - ter,

`Am*`　`(N.C.)`　　`E7`
God's gonna trouble the water.

[*cut this chord short, N.C. = no chord]

CHAPTER 6:
FINGERPICKING AND MELODIC PLAYING

In this chapter we will look beyond strumming. The fingers can be used individually to create interesting accompaniments and to play melodies.

FINGERPICKING: FIRST STEPS

All the material we have seen so far has focused on strumming. The ukulele's four strings can be played individually too, whether to play melodies (which we will look at later) or to play chord notes in musically interesting patterns.

If you have been using a pick up to this point, it's time to put it down and start using your fingers. Fingerpicking on the ukulele has some things in common with both classical playing and folk fingerpicking on the guitar, so if you know anything about either of these you will have a head start.

Although in principle any right-hand finger can be used to play any string, let's start with the basic technique that is used most of the time. The thumb and first three fingers cover one string each. We will use the same terminology as classical guitar.

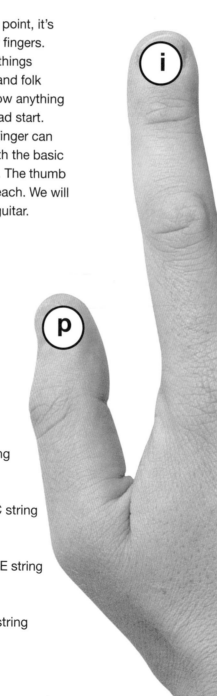

 thumb (*pulgar*) – plays G string

 index finger (*indice*) – plays C string

middle finger (*medio*) – plays E string

ring finger (*anular*) – plays A string

EXERCISES

Each of these exercises consists of a repetitive fingerpicking pattern using a single chord. These patterns are some of the building blocks of the fingerpicking style. Don't worry about rhythms for now: just keep repeating the pattern, aiming for an even flow. All notes should be allowed to ring on for as long as possible – ideally until the same string is played again.

Fingerpicking
The right hand in position for fingerpicking. Many patterns are played using one finger per string as shown opposite.

1. G

p	i	m	a		p	i	m	a		p	i	m	a		p	i	m	a
1	2	3	4		1	2	3	4		1	2	3	4		1	2	3	4

2. F

p	a	m	i		p	a	m	i		p	a	m	i		p	a	m	i
1	2	3	4		1	2	3	4		1	2	3	4		1	2	3	4

3. C

p	m	i	a		p	m	i	a		p	m	i	a		p	m	i	a
1	2	3	4		1	2	3	4		1	2	3	4		1	2	3	4

4. Am

p	a	i	m		p	a	i	m		p	a	i	m		p	a	i	m
1	2	3	4		1	2	3	4		1	2	3	4		1	2	3	4

5. Dm

a	m	i	p		a	m	i	p		a	m	i	p		a	m	i	p
1	2	3	4		1	2	3	4		1	2	3	4		1	2	3	4

INTRODUCING NOTATION & TABLATURE

Fingerpicking and melodic playing cannot easily be represented using the sort of notation encountered up to this point. Ukulele music can be notated using standard musical notation as used for other instruments, and also tablature, a special form of notation used for guitar and other instruments.

STANDARD NOTATION

All instruments in Western music share the system of standard musical notation. This means that it is possible to play music written for the violin or flute (for example) on the ukulele, as long as you know where to find the notes.

Standard notation uses a system of five lines called a stave, and the spaces between them, to show the pitches of notes, together with a system of notating rhythm.

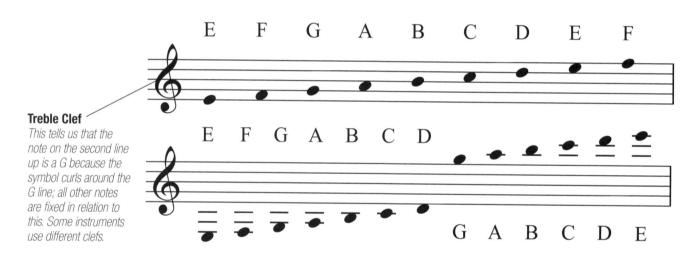

Treble Clef
This tells us that the note on the second line up is a G because the symbol curls around the G line; all other notes are fixed in relation to this. Some instruments use different clefs.

Notes above and below this range are shown using temporary lines called leger lines – as many as necessary.

NOTE DURATIONS

Symbol	American	British	Duration in
o	Whole note	Semibreve	4 beats
𝅗𝅥	Half note	Minim	2 beats
♩	Quarter note	Crotchet	1 beat
♪	Eighth note	Quaver	½ beat

In **4/4**, note durations are shown as follows:
Consecutive quavers (half beats) are usually beamed together in groups of two or four:

There is also a system of symbols telling us not to play for a given amount of time. These are called rests:

RESTS

Symbol	American	British	Duration in
—	Whole note	Semibreve	4 beats
—	Half note	Minim	2 beats
⅄	Quarter note	Crotchet	1 beat
⅂	Eighth note	Quaver	½ beat

TABLATURE

On many instruments, there is only one way to play any given note. On fretted stringed instruments, however, it can be hard to know where to play any given note, as the same note can often be found in more than one place. The system known as tablature (often abbreviated to 'tab') displays notes in terms of their physical location on the instrument. For the ukulele, there are four horizontal lines (one for each string); numbers represent fret numbers.

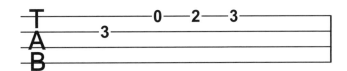

The example above consists of four notes: E string, 3rd fret followed by three notes on the A string: open, 2nd fret and 3rd fret.

Although tablature is useful for telling us where to find notes, it tells us nothing about the rhythm or note names. Standard notation and tablature are often used together when writing for fretted instruments.
Here we have the same notes. The top stave tells us that the notes are G, A, B and C. It also tells us the rhythm: 1, 2 & 3 (with a rest on 4).

Rest
Nothing is to be played on the fourth note, keeping to the count of 4/4.

MORE FINGERPICKING

Let's explore some more fingerpicking patterns. Each exercise here uses a repeated picking pattern throughout, with a few slight variations, over a changing chord sequence. Make sure you observe the picking shown throughout. To help with the rhythm, the counting is also shown between the staves.

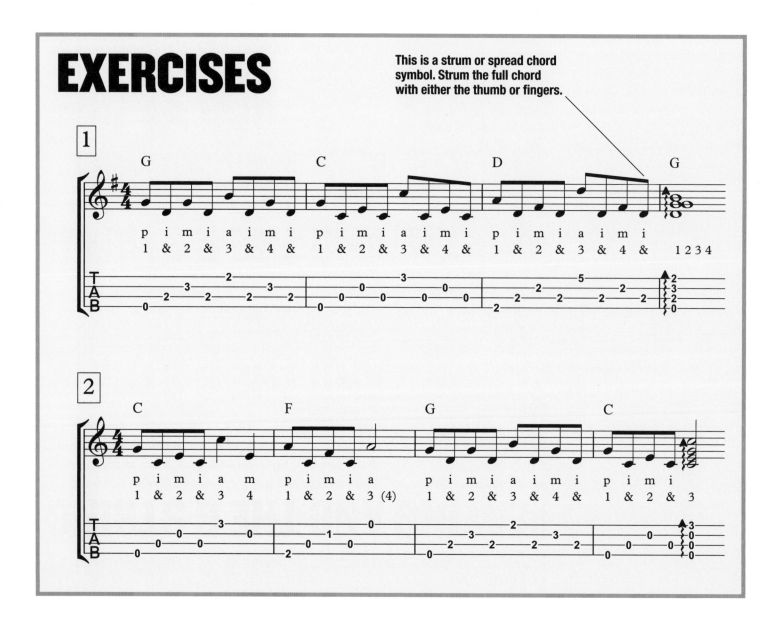

MELODIC PLAYING

So far we have focused on various types of accompaniment: strumming and picking. The uke can also be used to play melodically. A basic grasp of musical notation and/or tablature is very helpful here if you want to be able to read tunes from a variety of printed sources; you could also try working out some tunes for yourself.

Single-note melodies may be played either using the pick or the fingers. There are no strict rules governing which right-hand fingers to use; some players alternate the first two fingers (i and m), while others use the thumb and index finger in a similar way.

The exercises here all use note values introduced earlier in this chapter, and stay within first position. This means that the left hand should cover one fret per finger. At this level, take the rhythmic information from the note values, and use the TAB stave to tell you where to play each note.

Left hand covering first position
In first position, the first finger plays any notes at the first fret, the second finger covers the second fret, and so on.

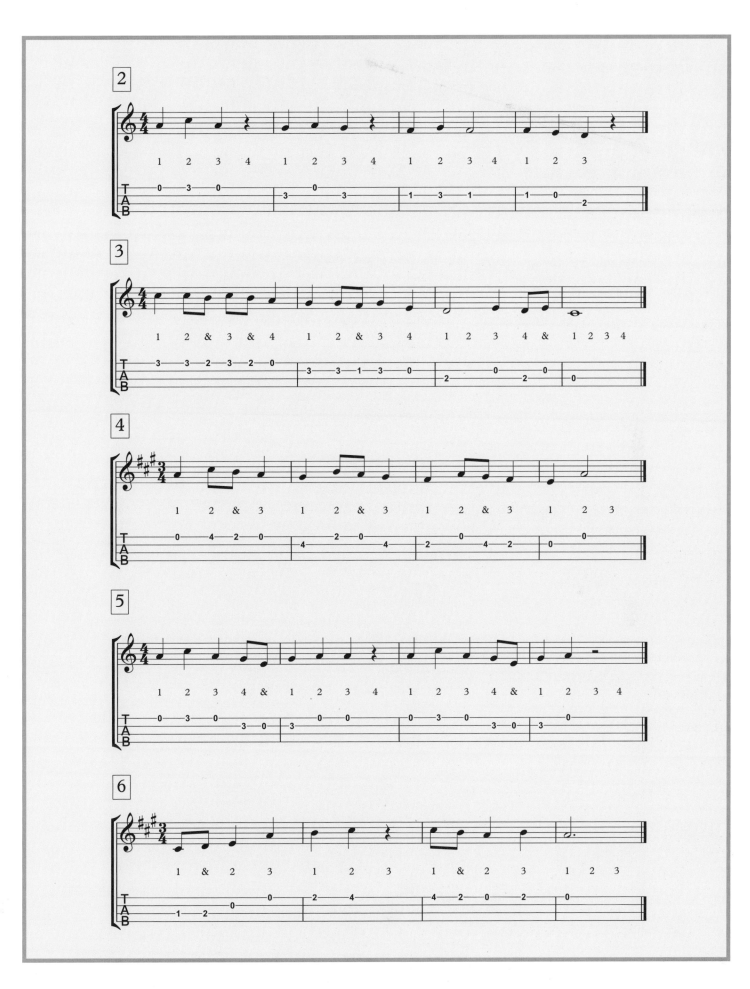

MORE MELODIC PLAYING AND SCALES

When attempting to find tunes on the ukulele, it helps to have a grasp of a few basics. For most music, the major scale is an important building block. This is the set of notes also known as 'do, re, mi, fa, so, la, ti, do'. In simple terms, a major scale is a way of playing all the notes found in a given major key; so, for example, a basic melody in C major contains only notes from the C major scale.

THE C MAJOR SCALE – FIRST POSITION
The C major scale can be found in first position, using both fretted notes and open strings. The usual way to notate and practise a scale is to play all the way from the lowest note to the highest and back down again.

TRANSPOSING THE SCALE
Like chords, scale shapes can also be transposed if they include only fretted notes. To transpose the C major scale up by a tone (from C to D), we have to move not only the fretted notes, but also the open strings. This results in a scale shape in second position – so the first finger plays notes at the second fret, and the other fingers play one fret each above this. This scale shape is moveable; so, for example, we can start at the fifth fret for an F major scale.

F MAJOR

D MAJOR

94

MELODIC PLAYING AND THE G STRING

You may have noticed that these scales don't use the G string. This is because of the ukulele's re-entrant tuning: the open G string is actually the same note as the E string, third fret. Any notes in a given position on the G string can usually be found more easily on other strings. This is not to say that the G string can't be used for melodic playing, as we will see on p. 107.

EXERCISES

These exercises use the 1st position C major scale shape and the moveable major scale shape, first in D major and then in F major.

BRITTNI PAIVA
1988–

RECOMMENDED LISTENING:

"Take Five"
"Europa"
"Summertime"

Brittni Paiva is a Hawaiian virtuoso ukulele player. Starting as a talented multi-instrumentalist and something of a child prodigy, Paiva 'found her instrument' when she branched out to the uke at the age of eleven. Since then she has produced half a dozen albums. On her first album she played ukulele, bass and slack key guitar (another characteristically Hawaiian instrument).

Brittni Paiva's music transcends stylistic boundaries, often incorporating elements of Electronic Dance Music (EDM) alongside styles as diverse as flamenco, gypsy jazz and Israeli music. She has pioneered the use of looper pedals with the ukulele, and remixed tracks by other acts. These allow arrangements with complex textures to be built up one layer at a time by a single musician.

Paiva has appeared with many high-profile musicians during their visits to Hawaii, including Tommy Emmanuel and Carlos Santana, and she frequently plays concerts throughout the US and beyond.

Unusually, Paiva uses a thumb pick. This device (normally used by banjo players and fingerpicking country guitar players) wraps around the thumb to provide a picking surface but, unlike a regular pick, it does not interfere with fingerpicking.

New Generation
Brittni Paiva represents an exciting new generation of uke players – watch this space!

FAVOURED INSTRUMENT:

**KAMAKA CUSTOM
TENOR**

PLAY A SONG

Scarborough Fair

This traditional English song was a huge hit for Simon & Garfunkel and remains a favourite among folk singers to this day. Our version uses a fingerpicking accompaniment, which we have written out in full.

CHORDS

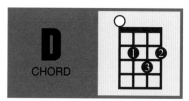

CHORD SEQUENCE

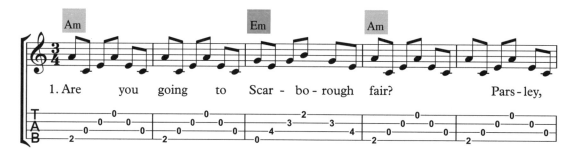

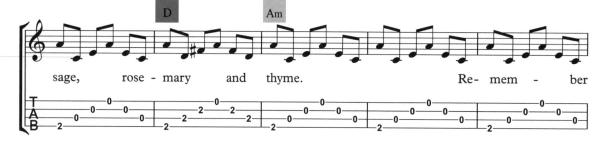

me   to   one who lives   there,   She   once

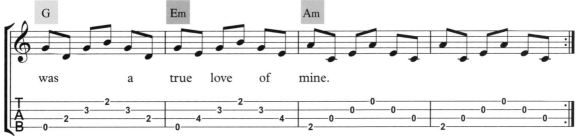

was   a   true   love   of   mine.

VERSE 2

Am   **Em**   **Am**
Tell her to make me a cambric shirt,

            D   **Am**
Parsley, sage rosemary and thyme.

        G   **Em**
Without a seam or needlework,

Am   **G**   **Em**   **Am**
Then she'll be a true love of mine.

VERSE 3

Am   **Em**   **Am**
Tell her to find me an acre of land,

            D   **Am**
Parsley, sage rosemary and thyme.

        G   **Em**
Between the salt water and the sea strand,

Am   **G**   **Em**   **Am**
Then she'll be a true love of mine.

CHAPTER 7:

ADVANCED TECHNIQUES

In this chapter, we will explore various techniques used on the uke and other fretted instruments to create more interesting, varied and fluid ideas.

LEFT: Tiny Tim (1932–1996) was an American singer and ukulele player who played the ukulele left-handed. He played a vintage Martin, a Favilla and a Johnston metal resonator.

COMBINING TECHNIQUES

So far we have looked at various types of playing in isolation (strumming, fingerpicking and melodic playing). Most real-world playing combines many techniques: for example, you might play the melody as an introduction, fingerpick the verses and strum the choruses of a song. The exercises here are designed to simulate this experience.

EXERCISES

Our first exercises combine picking on the G string with strumming on the remaining three strings (although you can strum all four if you wish). The thumb plays the G string while the remaining fingers do the strumming.

Exercise 2 combines picking and strumming in a different way. Pick the individual notes using the fingers p i m a a as usual, but play the strums using the thumb. The C major seventh chord is new, but it is a very simple shape using just a single finger at the second fret of the A string.

102

Exercise 3 combines melodic picking with a single strum in each bar. Experiment with different right-hand fingerings for the picked notes; the strums may be played using either the thumb or the fingers.

Exercise 4 uses a syncopated rhythm. The picked notes fall on the beat (1 and 3), while the strums are on offbeats. If you find this challenging, you could try a 'fake' strum instead: simply pick all three strings almost simultaneously (using fingers i, m and a).

ADVANCED LEFT-HAND TECHNIQUES

The techniques here all provide ways to achieve a more fluid sound on the uke. So far, we have picked or strummed every individual note or chord. Pull-offs, hammer-ons and slides are all about getting more notes from the instrument every time you pick.

HAMMER-ON

As the name suggests, this technique involves 'hammering' a left-hand finger on to the fretboard to produce a new note on a string that is already sounding. The first note may be either an open string or a fretted note. The hammer-on needs to have enough force to keep the note sounding.

Hammer-on from open string

First, play the open string. Next, hammer the finger on to the string at the desired fret in order to change the sounding note.

PULL-OFF

This is like a hammer-on in reverse. After playing a fretted note, the fretting finger is literally pulled off the string to change the pitch to a lower note. This can be either an open string or a lower fretted note. Rather than just removing the finger, there has to be a slight plucking motion so that the string is re-energized to produce the second note. This can take some practice.

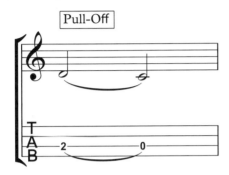

Hammer-on between fretted notes (below)
Play the first fretted note, then hammer-on with another finger at a higher fret.

SLIDE

This is a simple technique that involves changing the pitch of a note while it is sounding. Simply play the first note, and then slide the finger up or down the string to the desired target note.

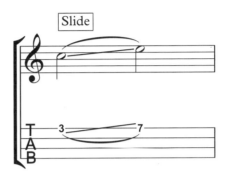

Slide (below)
The fretting finger slides up or down the string to change the pitch of a sounding note. Finger pressure must be maintained to keep the note sounding.

EXERCISES

These exercises incorporate hammer-ons and pull-offs into fingerpicking patterns.

1

2

3

4

EXERCISES

CAMPANELLA STYLE

This is a fingerpicking style in which melodies are played in a different way. Rather than using adjacent notes on the same string, consecutive notes are always played on different strings. All notes should be allowed to ring on for as long as possible. The G string really comes into its own in this style, as its tuning makes it easy to insert melodic notes that alternate with notes on other strings; using the thumb for this helps to maintain a fluid line.

PLAY A SONG

Down By The Riverside

This simple spiritual song can be interpreted in a number of ways. You could just apply a fast strumming pattern, but to add more interest you could also combine strumming and picking.

SUGGESTED PICKING PATTERN

The suggested pattern involves a strum on beat 2. If you find you struggle to indicate this, you could try a 'fake' strum instead (fingerpicking each string in rapid succession). Beat 3 uses a hammer-on from the open string to the chord note. We have only shown the F chord pattern – you will need to adapt this idea to the other chords in the song.

CHORDS

SUGGESTED STRUMMING PATTERN

VERSE

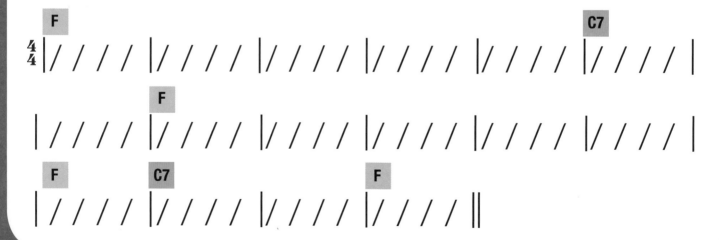

CHORUS

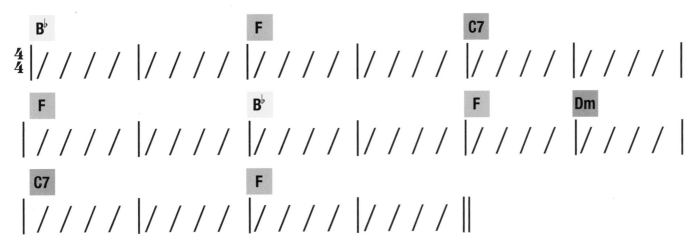

VERSE 1

F

Gonna lay down my burden, Down by the riverside,

C7

   Down by the riverside,

F

   Down by the riverside.

Gonna lay down my burden, Down by the riverside,

C7   **F**

   Down by the riverside.

CHORUS

        B♭

I ain't gonna study war no more,

        F

Ain't gonna study war no more,

        C7   **F**

I ain't gonna study war no more.

        B♭

I ain't gonna study war no more,

        F   **Dm**

Ain't gonna study war no more,

        C7   **F**

I ain't gonna study war no more.

VERSE 2

I'm gonna lay down my sword and shield…

Repeat Chorus

VERSE 3

I'm gonna put on my long white robe…

Repeat Chorus

VERSE 4

I'm gonna try on my starry crown…

Repeat Chorus

VERSE 5

I'm gonna talk with the prince of peace…

Repeat Chorus

CHAPTER 8:

TIPS AND TRICKS

In this chapter we explore some techniques and ideas beyond ordinary strumming and picking that can lend your playing a more advanced quality.

LEFT: Pearl Jam frontman Eddie Vedder released a solo album called *Ukulele Songs*. It consisted of original songs and covers.

ADVANCED TECHNIQUES

Many contemporary solo ukulele players use a range of techniques to add unusual textures and a sense of performance and fun. Incorporating these alongside more conventional techniques can really broaden the possibilities of the instrument.

PERCUSSION

The ukulele's hollow wooden body makes a very effective percussion instrument. Both hands can be used in any number of ways.

Right-hand tap
Here the right hand is used to drum on the uke's lower body. A variety of sounds can be produced using the thumb or fingers either apart or together.

TAPPED NOTES

As well as picking and strumming conventionally, the right hand can also be used to produce notes more directly, by tapping forcibly on the string so it produces a note when it hits the fretboard. This technique requires precision, particularly for large hands playing a soprano uke.

Left-hand tap
Here the left hand taps the upper body. The right hand can be used to mute the strings to prevent them from sounding accidentally.

Thrumming
The right hand fingers are flicked outwards in rapid succession to create an effective variation on conventional strumming.

SYMBOLS

There are various ways to show these techniques in notation and tab. Usually, percussion is shown using 'crossed' note heads (crosses instead of conventional note heads) along with some explanation. Tapping is shown using the note produced plus some additional symbol such as '+' or 'T'.

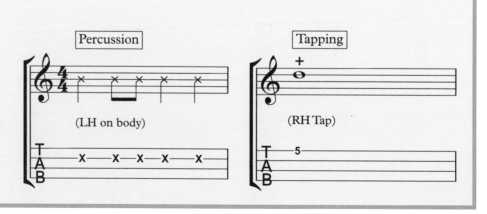

EXERCISES

1: Strums alternating with RH taps.

2: '+' symbol indicated RH taps. Other hammer-ons/pull-offs are LH. The chords should ring on for a full bar.

3: Ukulele drumming variations: these simple beats can be used as a starting point for exploring the percussive possibilities of the ukulele. Repeat each section slowly until you are comfortable before increasing the speed, then try mixing them up and adding variations of your own. In the third section, try using the RH first finger to tap the strings instead of the body.

EXPLORING CHORD FLAVOURS

So far we have seen major, minor and seventh chords, but there are many other kinds of chords to explore. Here are a few interesting ones, presented as both open shapes (with open strings) and also moveable shapes.

B♭maj7
Open
CHORD

B♭maj7

Bmaj7
Moveable
CHORD

Bmaj7

Am7
Open
CHORD

Am7

UKULELE TIP: Any shape consisting of fretted notes only can be transposed up the fretboard, and most open shapes can be transposed with the addition of a barre or fourth fretted note. So if you know a shape for Cmaj7, for example, you can easily find Dmaj7, Emaj7 and so on. The important thing is to know how far to move the shape. Simply count two frets for each consecutive note name (A–B, C–D etc), except for B–C and E–F, which are only one fret apart. The note names repeat after G, so A is two frets above G, and names with sharps or flats (#/♭) are found in between (so B♭ is found between A and B, and F# is found between F and G).

Bm7
Moveable
CHORD

Bm7

Open strings

C6
Open
CHORD

C6

D6
Moveable
CHORD

D6

Gdim7
Open
CHORD

Gdim7

Adim7
Moveable
CHORD

Adim7

FUN WITH TUNINGS

So far we have been using 'standard' ukulele tuning. This is actually only one of many possible ways to tune the instrument. Each tuning has its own unique flavour, making different sonorities and textures available. Let's explore a few of these.

OPEN CHORD TUNINGS

This involves tuning the strings to the notes of a chord. If you know the notes that make up the chord you are trying to use, the simplest approach is to tune each string to the chord note nearest to its usual pitch. You can check which notes you need by referring to 'Building A Chord' on p. 53. The easiest chord tuning to start with is open C tuning: simply drop the pitch of the A string by a tone to G. This is really easy to achieve as it is the same pitch as the regular G string.

The great thing about this tuning is that any major chord can be played using just a single finger barring across all strings. In C tuning, the most important chords in the key of C can be found using all the open strings (C), barring at the fifth fret (F) and at the seventh fret (G).

'GUITAR' TUNING

Standard uke tuning is essentially based on the top four strings of guitar tuning, except that the absolute pitch is a fourth higher (like a guitar with a capo at the fifth fret) and the G string is raised by an octave. Some players prefer to tune the G string to the lower octave, so that the tuning is exactly like the guitar but higher. This has two advantages: guitarists are used to the 'lowest' note in the chord actually being the lowest-sounding. Also, this makes melodies easier to find.

A standard G string will not sound good if it is tuned down by an octave – you will need a thicker-gauge string for this purpose.

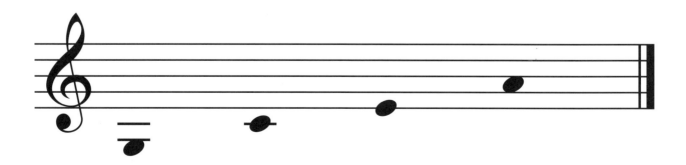

VIOLIN TUNING (FIFTHS)

If you play the violin, you could try tuning the uke like one, making it easy to play any melody you know on the violin. This involves tuning in fifths (so the strings are five scale steps apart). The mandolin is also tuned like this, so a violin-tuned uke will sound a lot like a mandolin.

The violin is tuned G D A E.

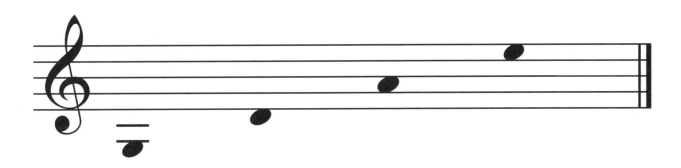

This results in completely different chord shapes. Here are a few useful chords to get you started.

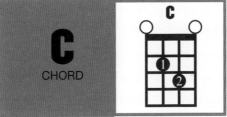

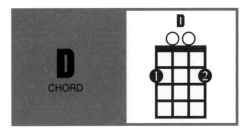

UKULELE TIP: If you are interested in the origins of the ukulele, you could investigate tunings associated with its ancestor instruments, such as the machete and cavaquinho. The latter is usually tuned D G B D; this non-re-entrant tuning requires the use of a heavier bottom string.

STRING BREAKAGE

Tuning any string too much higher than its usual pitch can result in breakage. If you plan to get really experimental with tunings, you should probably buy a lot of spare strings. If your desired tuning causes a string to break, try the same thing with a lighter gauge.

PLAY A SONG

Old Folks At Home

This classic Stephen Foster song (also known as "Swanee River") is now the official song of the State of Florida. Our version is a fingerpicking arrangement where the melody is incorporated into the pattern.

This uses Campanella style (p. 107) to a degree, though not strictly. In general, just three easy chord shapes are needed (C, F and G), with a few extra notes used to bring out the melody. These are all found in first position except for the highest note ("All the WORLD"), where the fourth finger should be used to play a high D at the fifth fret. All the notes in each bar should ring on for as long as possible.

UKULELE HEROES

GEORGE FORMBY

1904–1961

RECOMMENDED LISTENING:
"The Window Cleaner" (also known as "When I'm Cleaning Windows")
"Leaning On A Lamp Post"
"With My Little Stick Of Blackpool Rock"

George Formby was an English singer, comedian and actor. During the height of his fame in the years around World War II, he was the UK's highest-paid entertainer and achieved international fame both with recordings and film appearances.

Born in Lancashire as the son of a successful singer and music hall entertainer (George Formby Senior), the young George began to appear in silent films (though his father would have preferred him to have taken a 'proper' job) and took to the stage in the early 1920s around the time of his father's death. He would soon eclipse his father's fame, in part because of the new possibilities offered by both film and recording. Having already established a film career as a comic actor in the 1930s, by the time of World War II Formby was the perfect morale-boosting entertainer, representing working-class stoicism and cheeky Northern humour.

Unusually for a performer of his era, Formby co-wrote many of his most famous songs, including the iconic "The Window Cleaner". During the 1920s, 30s and 40s, he released dozens of songs, many associated with film releases. In Britain, Formby is inextricably linked in the popular consciousness with the ukulele, though he in fact generally played a banjolele (essentially a ukulele with a banjo body). His accompaniment style was simple but energetic, and he played an important role in popularizing the instrument in Britain. The Beatles made several references to him; the young John Lennon learned to play the ukulele before moving on to the guitar, and George Harrison remained an enthusiastic champion (of both Formby and the ukulele) until the end of his life.

FAVOURED INSTRUMENT

BANJOLELE
(LUDWIG AND DALLAS)

National Celebrity
George Formby was a national celebrity in Britain, and one of the first such entertainers to write some of his own material.

PLAYING WITH OTHERS

Although the ukulele is a great instrument for a solo musician, it can be the perfect addition to a band or other ensemble. Playing with others can be hugely rewarding, but can also come with its own frustrations and many new aspects to think about.

AMPLIFICATION

The ukulele works well with other acoustic instruments such as acoustic guitar, violin and banjo. In this context, and in small venues, the uke may sound great without any kind of amplification. However, if you want to combine the ukulele with instruments such as electric guitar, drums and keyboards, you may well need some form of amplification.

The simplest way to amplify the ukulele is to use a microphone connected to a PA system. This means that you don't have to modify the instrument or invest in a dedicated amp. The disadvantage is that you have no freedom to move on stage.

Another option is to use a pickup. There are various types of pickup available that can be attached to any acoustic instrument. Alternatively, you could get a ukulele with an integrated pickup. This could be a standard acoustic ukulele with a pickup, or else a 'mini electric guitar' model. Depending on your choice and the sound you are trying to achieve, this could be connected to a PA system, a dedicated acoustic instrument amp or an electric guitar amp.

UKE ORCHESTRA/ENSEMBLE

This type of group has become very popular in recent years. Finding or starting one can be a great way to learn

Zooey Deschanel (She & Him)
Zooey's amplified electric uke works well together with electric guitar, bass and drums in a rock line-up.

from other players. The emphasis is usually on fun rather than virtuoso musicianship. The key to the success of a uke ensemble is to develop effective arrangements. This means that everyone should not play the same thing. It is also useful if there are some bigger ukes involved, all the way down to a bass uke, so a wider frequency range is covered. Some uke ensembles compromise on this and use a double bass or acoustic bass guitar instead.

ARRANGING

When conceiving an arrangement for uke ensemble, try to incorporate some or all of the techniques covered in this book. One or more players could play the melody while others play the chords and the bass instrument plays the bass line. Even within the rhythm players, you could have some players strumming and others fingerpicking. Also, try to vary the role of each player – it's more interesting to have various different types of playing within one song.

Ukulele Society of America
Like the Ukulele Orchestra of Great Britain, its US counterpart has helped inspire a new generation to take up the uke.

Tuner
Tuning to a common reference is important. There's no excuse for everyone in your band not to have their own inexpensive clip tuner, like this one.

TUNING

When playing on your own, the uke just has to be in tune with itself – it doesn't matter if it's a little bit sharp or flat as a whole. When playing with others, however, it is crucial for everyone to tune to a common reference: make sure that everyone is using a tuner, and that all tuners are set to 'A=440Hz'.

RECORDING

There are many reasons you might want to record your playing. For one thing, it's a great way to get a clear view of your progress as a player. Listening to yourself can be highly revealing (and sometimes depressing, but usually constructive). You might also want to record your band or ukulele ensemble.

HARDWARE

To make a simple recording, the best thing is to use a dedicated solid state recorder with an integrated microphone. These generally record to SD card or internal memory, and recordings can be transferred to your

Avid Pro Tools
Above: Avid's Pro Tools is one of the industry standards in multi-track recording software. It is available in many configurations to suit anyone from a home-based hobbyist to high-end commercial studios.

Headphones
Headphones are essential for any kind of multi-track recording, allowing you to hear existing tracks without these spilling on to the new track you are recording.

Handy Hardware
A basic mixer may be a useful addition to a computer recording set-up. A mixer processes sound so you can equalize it – highs, mids and lows – as well as add effects (echo, reverb, delay).

The Missing Link
This basic audio interface acts as a bridge between your uke and computer.

computer for editing. If you are recording yourself singing and playing, the only way to adjust the recorded balance between the two (apart from adjusting the actual volume of your singing and playing, of course) is to adjust the position and orientation of the microphone.

For more sophisticated recording capability, you will need all or most of the following:

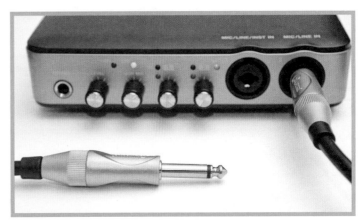

- A computer (Mac/PC) or tablet
- An audio interface
- One or more microphones
- Recording software

COMPUTER OR TABLET

Almost any computer or tablet (or even smartphone) will be capable of running some sort of recording software; more powerful machines will be able to run powerful professional software, while tablets generally lack sufficient power.

Although it is possible to use your computer or tablet's integrated audio connections, for better results you will need some form of audio interface.

AUDIO INTERFACE

This is simply a box connected to your computer or tablet to provide audio connections: from one input and one output to hundreds of channels, depending on your requirements and budget. It is important to check whether your chosen interface is compatible with your hardware and operating system, and that it has the right inputs and outputs for you: in particular, you will probably want at least one microphone input; many interfaces also have line inputs and high impedance ('hi-Z') inputs for direct connection of electro-acoustic instruments.

MICROPHONES

You can record the uke by pointing a relatively inexpensive dynamic microphone such as a Shure SM57 at it, but a condenser microphone (usually a little more expensive) will often give better results. This could also be useful for recording other acoustic instruments and vocals.

SOFTWARE

There are many free or inexpensive apps for simple recording. For more advanced recording, editing and mixing (including multi-track recording and integrated virtual instruments and effects), you will need a piece of software called a Digital Audio Workstation (usually abbreviated to DAW). As well as the full, professional versions of these programs, many are available in 'lite' versions, most of which are still surprisingly powerful. Examples include:

- Avid Pro Tools
- Apple Logic Pro
- PreSonus Studio One

CHAPTER 9:

CHORD
REFERENCE

This chapter is a library of chords arranged logically to provide beginners with a convenient reference point. It collects together the chords you need to play more of the kinds of songs found in this book.

LEFT: Australian Singer-songwriter Vance Joy wrote his hit song 'Riptide' on a ukulele, which he has enjoyed playing since childhood.

C CHORDS

C

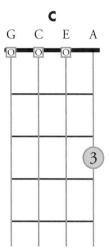

C

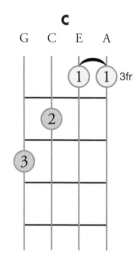

C7

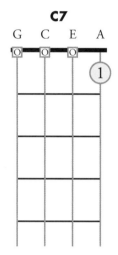

Cmaj7

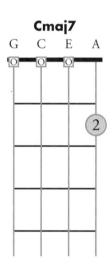

Cm

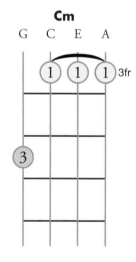

Cm

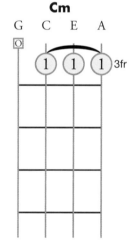

Cm7

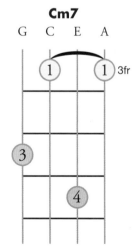

C6

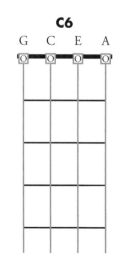

C9

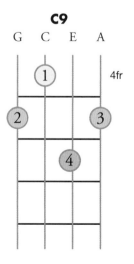

C#/Db CHORDS

C#
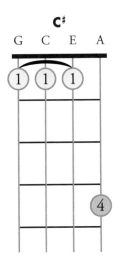

C#
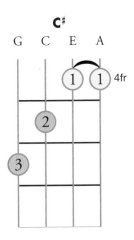

C#7
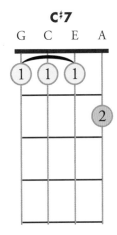

C#maj7
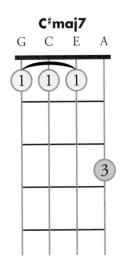

C#m
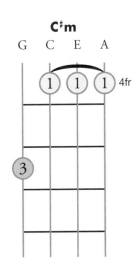

C#m
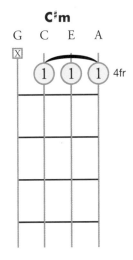

C#m7
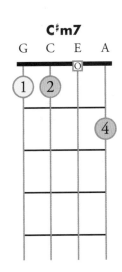

C#6
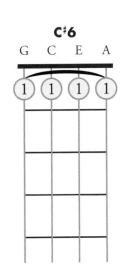

C#9
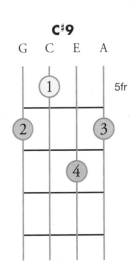

D CHORDS

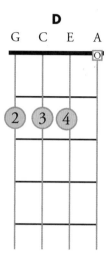

① = FIRST FINGER   ② = SECOND FINGER   ③ = THIRD FINGER   ④ = FOURTH FINGER   O = OPEN STRING   X = DO NOT PLAY THIS STRING

D
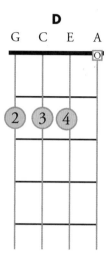

D
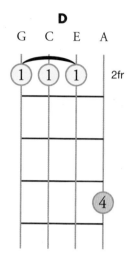

D7
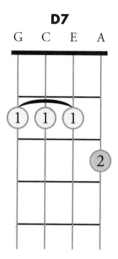

Dmaj7
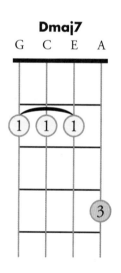

Dm
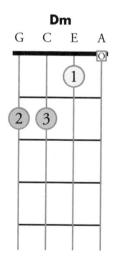

Dm
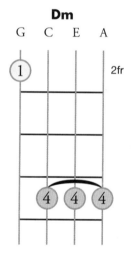

Dm7
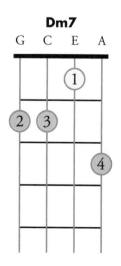

D6
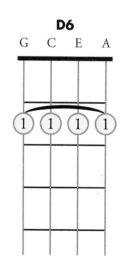

D9
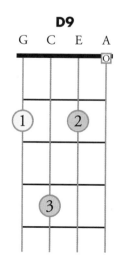

E♭ CHORDS

E♭
G C E A
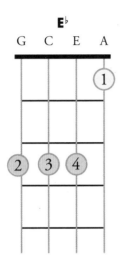

E♭
G C E A
3fr
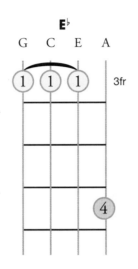

E♭7
G C E A
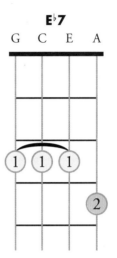

E♭maj7
G C E A
3fr
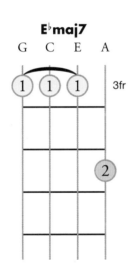

E♭m
G C E A
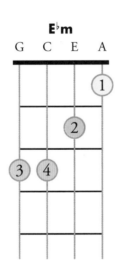

E♭m
G C E A
3fr
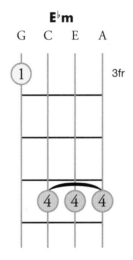

E♭m7
G C E A
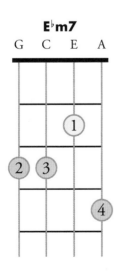

E♭6
G C E A
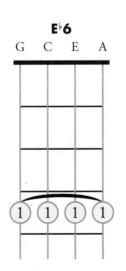

E♭9
G C E A
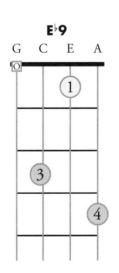

E CHORDS

① = FIRST FINGER ② = SECOND FINGER ③ = THIRD FINGER ④ = FOURTH FINGER O = OPEN STRING X = DO NOT PLAY THIS STRING

E
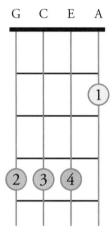

E
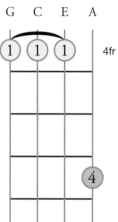

E7
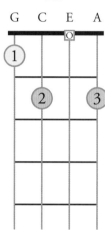

Emaj7
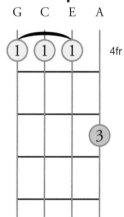

Em
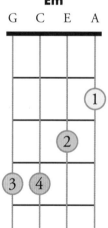

Em
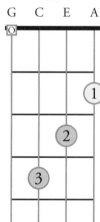

Em7
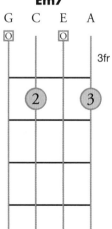

E6
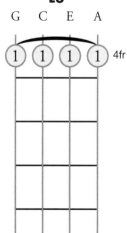

E9
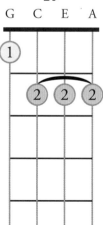

F CHORDS

F

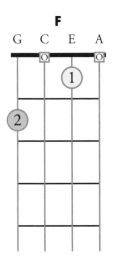

F

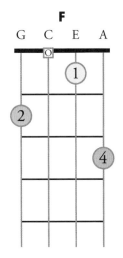

F7

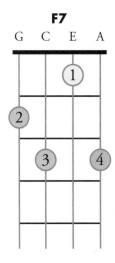

Fmaj7

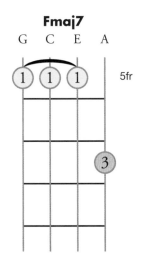

Fm

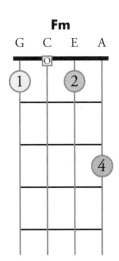

Fm

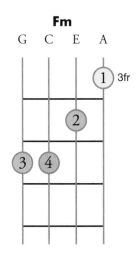

Fm7

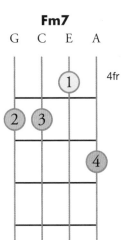

F6

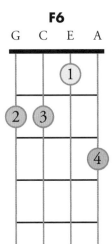

F9

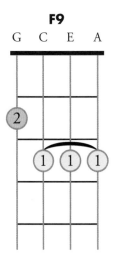

F#/Gb CHORDS

F#
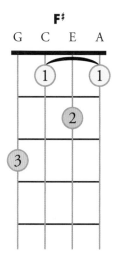

F#
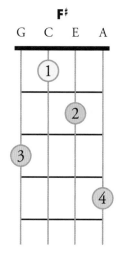

F#7
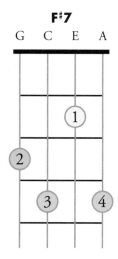

F#maj7
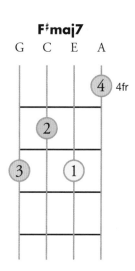

F#m
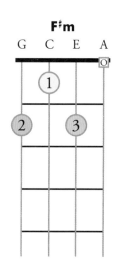

F#m
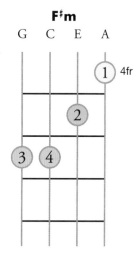

F#m7
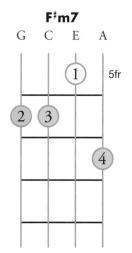

F#6
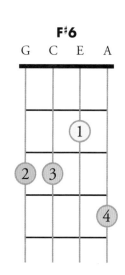

F#9
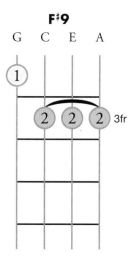

G CHORDS

G
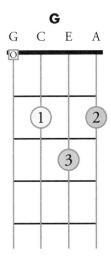

G
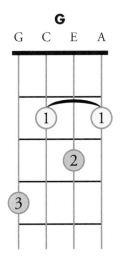

G7
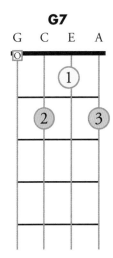

Gmaj7
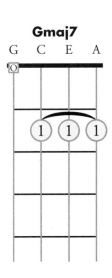

Gm
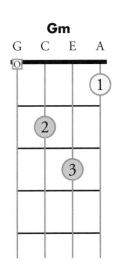

Gm
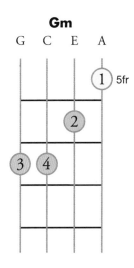

Gm7
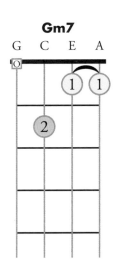

G6
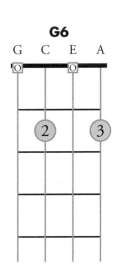

G9
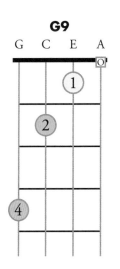

A♭/G♯ CHORDS

A♭
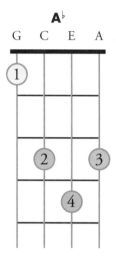

A♭
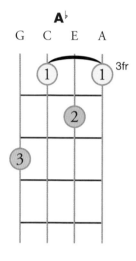

A♭7
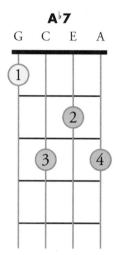

A♭maj7
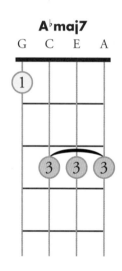

A♭m
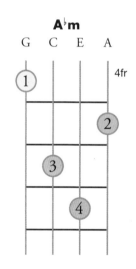

A♭m
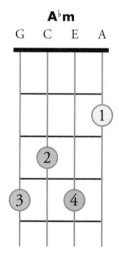

A♭m7
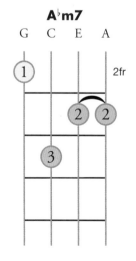

A♭6
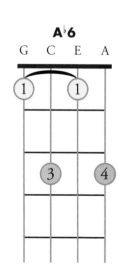

A♭9
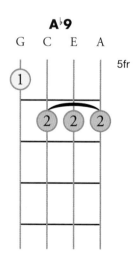

A CHORDS

A
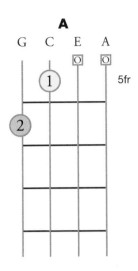

A
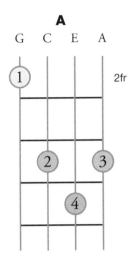

A7
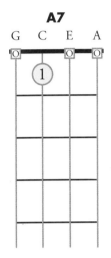

Amaj7
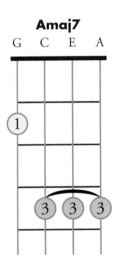

Am
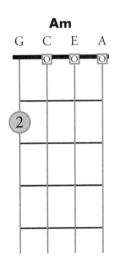

Am
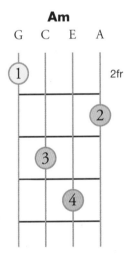

Am7
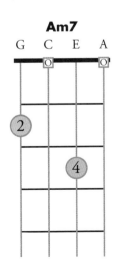

A6
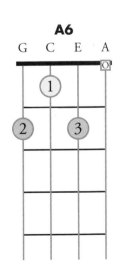

A9
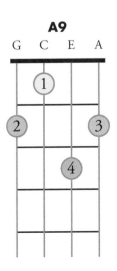

B♭ CHORDS

B♭
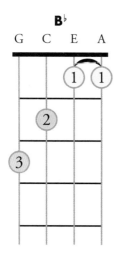

B♭
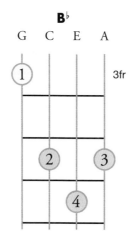

B♭7
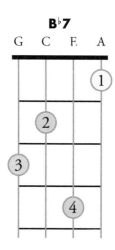

B♭maj7
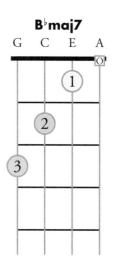

B♭m
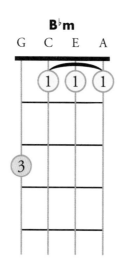

B♭m
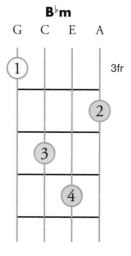

B♭m7
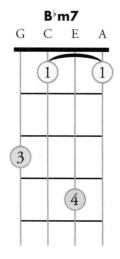

B♭6
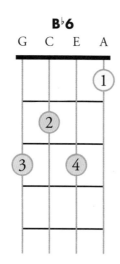

B♭9
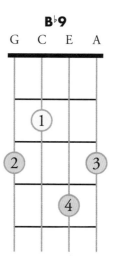

B CHORDS

B
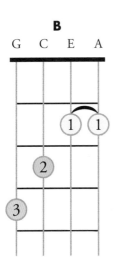

B
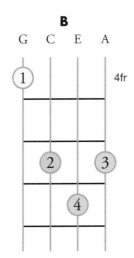

B7
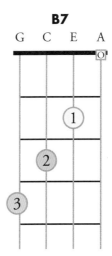

Bmaj7
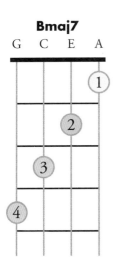

Bm
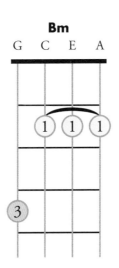

Bm
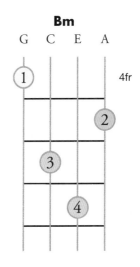

Bm7
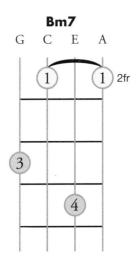

B6
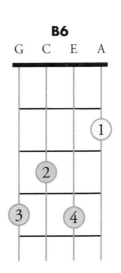

B9
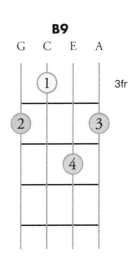

GLOSSARY

Accented Note
A note played with more emphasis than others.

Bar
A subdivision of time in music.

Barre
Using your finger to hold down more than one string at one fret in a single chord, in order to build chords using that fret as the 'nut'.

Bass
Sounds of a lower frequency.

Beat
A single pulse of rhythm.

Bend
Raising the pitch of a note by pushing the string sideways across the fretboard.

Body
The main part of a ukulele (excluding the neck). The part that contains the soundhole.

BPM
Beats Per Minute refers to the tempo of a song. It is expressed as a number that literally records the beats to count for every minute.

Bridge
The bridge is on the body of the ukulele and transfers sound from the strings to the body of the ukulele.

Capo
A device which clamps onto the fretboard to keep all the string down on the same fret. Essentially barring the strings on that particular fret with a capo instead of your finger.

Chord
Three or more pitches played simultaneously, usually a root, third and fifth.

Chord Progression
A sequence of chords played one after each other.

C (Common time)
The symbol "C" used as a time signature; another name for 4/4 time.

Downstroke
The part of a strumming pattern where your strumming hand is moving down the strings or away from you.

Ensemble
A group of musicians who perform together.

Flat
Flat generally just means lower. The flat of the note you are on would be one semitone lower. To tune flat, you tune 'down'.

Fingerpicking
A pattern-based way of playing through chord progressions using the fingers.

Fifth (note of a chord)
In a scale, the distance between a certain note and another note four notes above it. The certain note is counted as I, the note four notes above that is V.

Fretboard
The fretted surface of the neck where you press down the strings.

Fret
Technically, the frets are the small metal bars across the neck of your ukulele or bass. When you press your fingertip down between two 'frets' you will fret the string and make the appropriate corresponding note. (You do not press your fingertip 'on' the frets, but between them).

Hammer-On
The action of 'hammering down' a fretting finger on to a higher fret of a string that has just been plucked, creating a sudden change up in the note without plucking it again.

Harmony
Two or more pleasing notes sounding simultaneously.

Headstock
The headstock houses the tuning pegs that hold the strings in place.

In Tune
A note is in-tune when it matches the pitch of another note in the manner it is supposed to. When tuning a ukulele, strings are 'in tune' with each other when you can sound the same note on different strings and they sound the same. When playing a chord, a note is in tune if it sounds at the right interval from the other notes around it.

Key
The tonal center of a piece of music.

Major
This is a type of scale or chord that sounds bright, happy and upbeat. It has no flats in it.

Melody
A succession of musical notes played one after another (usually the most recognizable tune of a song).

Metronome
A device that creates a clicking sound that can be set to any beat to assist with timing of a musical piece.

Minor
This is a type of scale or chord that sounds dark, maybe sad and gloomy. Minor scales or chords do use flats.

Neck
The part of a ukulele that houses the fret board.

Nut
The nut is placed at the end of the fingerboard and controls the strings spacing, distance from the edge of the fingerboard and their height above the first fret.

Octave
An interval of 12 semitones.

Offbeat
A note occurring between the beats in a bar.

Open
A string played with no left hand finger fretting any note.

Open Chord
A chord that contains open strings.

Pentatonic Scale
A scale with only 5 tones. There are two standard pentatonic scales: major and minor.

Position
The four frets that your hand is over at any given time.

Pick
A small, triangular-shaped piece of plastic used for striking the ukulele strings with the hand.

Pitch
The frequency of a note (how high or low it sounds).

Rhythm
A sequence of events played with the right hand on a ukulele, which gives a piece of music a distinct beat.

Riff
A repeated sequence of notes, most common in rock and pop.

Root note
The note from which a scale or chord is based. The first note of a scale or chord.

Saddle
The saddle is part of the bridge and although on some stringed instruments it allows for adjustment of intonation, it is generally fixed on a ukulele.

Scale
A sequence of notes that defines a musical key.

Semitone
The smallest musical interval in modern Western music. There are two semitones in one whole tone.

Sharp
Sharp generally means higher. The sharp of the note you are on would be one semitone higher. To tune sharp, you tune 'up'.

Slotted Headstock
A traditional method of finishing the head of the ukulele. Rather than having tuning pegs running through the head from underneath a slotted headstock has the pegs running in to the instrument from the side, with the strings running in to the slots to be wound around the pegs.

Sound Hole
The hole in the centre of the soundboard that allows the sound to travel out of the ukulele.

Strumming
A technique where the right hand plays the notes of a chord simultaneously, either with down or up strokes.

Syncopation
Using accents on some of the weaker beats to create a more diverse rhythm.

Swing
A rhythm in music in which the downbeat is felt slightly longer than the upbeat (sometimes called a shuffle).

Tablature
A pictorial system of notation for ukulele music, showing six strings and fret positions.

Tempo
The overall speed of a piece of music.

Third (note of a chord)
In a scale, the distance between a certain note and another note two notes above it. The certain note is counted as I, the note two notes above that is iii.

Time Signature
The time signature describes how many beats are contained in each bar. Common time signatures are **4/4** (4 beats to the bar) and **3/4** (3 beats to the bar). The first number refers to the number of beats in the bar and the second number refers to the note value that represents one beat.

Tone
The combination of pitch, volume, sustain and sound character produced by a particular ukulele or ukulele equipment.

Tuning
Adjusting the tuning pegs until a particular string vibrates at the correct frequency, and sounds the proper note(s).

Tuning peg
A knob used to tighten or loosen a string. The effect is to raise or lower the pitch to bring the string into proper tune.

Upstroke
The part of a strumming pattern where your strumming hand is moving up the strings or moving towards you.

USEFUL WEBLINKS

www.ukulele-chords.com

www.ukulele-tabs.com

www.youtube.com/user/ukuleleunderground

www.youtube.com/user/TheUkuleleTeacher

INDEX

PICTURE CREDITS